WHAT HAVE YOU

LEFT BEHIND?

Bushra al-Maqtari is a writer and journalist who lives in Sanaa, Yemen. Her writings have appeared in various Arabic and international newspapers and magazines, including the *New York Times*. In 2013, she received the Françoise Giroud Award for Defence of Freedom and Liberties in Paris as well as the Leaders for Democracy Prize awarded by the Project on Middle East Democracy in Washington. In 2020, she was awarded the Johann-Philipp-Palm-Award for Freedom of Speech and Press, following on from the publication of *What Have You Left Behind?* with Ullstein Verlag in Germany.

Sawad Hussain is a translator from Arabic whose work has been recognized by English PEN, the Anglo-Omani Society and the Saif Ghobash Banipal Prize for Arabic Literary Translation, among others. She is a judge for the Palestine Book Awards. Her upcoming translations include *Black Foam* by Haji Jaber and *Edo's Souls by Stella Gaitano*. She has run translation workshops under the auspices of Shadow Heroes, Africa Writes, The British Library, the National Centre for Writing, the Shubbak Festival and the Yiddish Book Center. She was the 2022 translator in residence at the British Centre for Literary Translation.

'Bushra al-Maqtari's boundlessly humane project of collecting firsthand accounts to document the nearly decade-long Yemeni Civil War – and the West's complicity in it – is unblinking in its moral gaze. Every single voice collected in these pages is a blow to the heart. By the time I finished this book, I was consumed by sorrow and rage. This is an act of witnessing, and of making us engage in the witnessing of a disgraceful, criminal war that will shake your soul.'
— Neel Mukherjee, author of *A State of Freedom*

'An oral history of war's folly in the tradition of Svetlana Alexievich, as devastating as Goya or Picasso. Al-Maqtari summons us to witness the innocent lives lost, and the love that survives in their wake.'
— Matthieu Aikins, author of *The Naked Don't Fear the Water*

'Journalists covering war regularly claim their reporting gives "a voice to the voiceless ". *What Have You Left Behind?* demonstrates that survivors of Yemen's conflict are not voiceless, they are unheard. Bushra al-Maqtari brings a cacophony of voices from one of the world's most under-reported conflicts; voices that compel us to hear what war does to civilians living through it. *What Have You Left Behind?* is a disturbing, often evocative and emotional oral record of a war that most of us know little if anything about. This is not the sanitized, politicized version of the conflict debated in the power houses of far-off capitals. If you want to understand the true impact of war, brace yourself to hear these voices from Yemen.'
— Iona Craig, winner of the Orwell Prize for Journalism

'Bushra al-Maqtari's book is like a cry from those buried beneath rubble, those the world has forgotten, nobody hears, and nobody helps.'
— Ulf Kalkreuth, *Das Erste*

'When the fire of this war dies down, and the regional conflicting parties agree to a truce, and foreign entities are invited to rebuild the country, in those moments we will still have these heartrending stories, as a reminder of the sheer folly, empty grandeur and cold-blooded cruelty embodied by the war in Yemen.'
— *Qantara*

'Bushra al-Maqtari writes against forgetting... Her reports get under our skin, horrify, move us to tears. Free of theatricality, the writing simple and compassionate, they make clear what war really means.'
— Susanne El Khafif, Deutschland Radio

'Al-Maqtari's portraits are unsettling in their urgency, their need to make the world understand that the war in Yemen must not be forgotten... I would even dare to speak of a kind of dark poetry in al-Maqtari. Her language is nuanced and empathetic.'
— *Spiesser*

'What sets this book apart is its narrative style, without being a novel, and its means of recording and documentation, without actually being a written record or document. ... What we read is painful, but our knowledge is enriched by the facts presented, as well as our literary experience with its language, marked by the pulse of life and death.'
— *Al Quds*

'It is an attempt to put in words the way cluster bombs kill, and how it feels when your own children, siblings, or parents are torn apart by grenades, shredded by machine gun fire, crushed or buried beneath falling rubble.'
— Florian Keisinger, *Der Tagesspiegel*

Fitzcarraldo Editions

WHAT HAVE YOU
LEFT BEHIND?

VOICES FROM A FORGOTTEN WAR

BUSHRA AL-MAQTARI

Translated by
SAWAD HUSSAIN

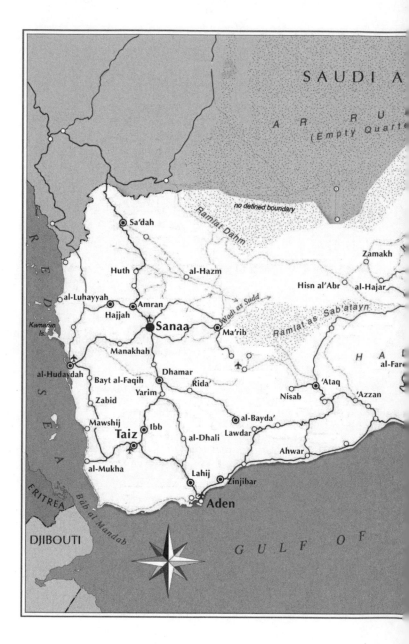

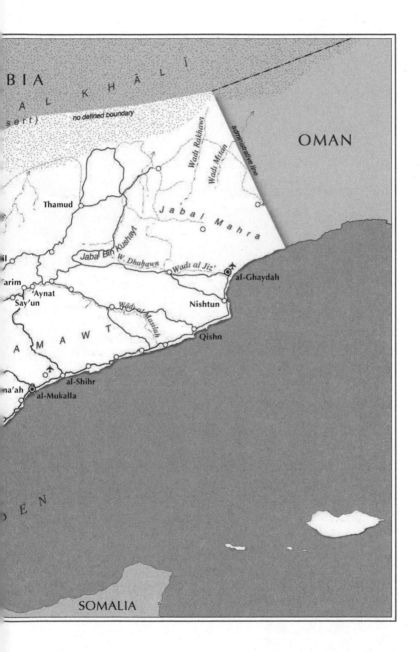

SOMEWHERE IN THE GLOBAL SOUTH

In my dreams, the war is silent. No missiles, no air raids, no murder, no famine, no fear, no hatred. But when I wake, the war is still raging, just as it has been the past four years. Air raids light up the Sanaa night sky; ambulance sirens pierce the quiet of night. And while I write, I think about the time it took for war to reach us.

After all, a war like this doesn't break out without warning; it takes a long time. A full turn of history. It took years, decades in fact, to push its way into our lives. I remember how its head drifted unmistakably towards us. It had been during the first weeks of March 2015, but our eyes weren't open wide enough to see it coming. Or maybe they were, but we didn't realize that what we were seeing were the harbingers of war. Houthi militia were on the streets, but it hadn't been anything like the day Sanaa had fallen a few months earlier.[1]

As night began, armoured vehicles and individuals in military fatigues holding weapons could be seen coming forth. These troops proceeded on the same desert roads used by ordinary travellers. I remember seeing military trucks rolling along the route from Sanaa to Aden. Slowly, they advanced through the mountain pass, blocking civilian traffic. The vehicles carried tanks that seemed fresh out of storage. Then a long line: rocket launchers, machine guns, more equipment, guarded by exhausted soldiers on foot. And even more trucks, this time with

1   On 21 September 2014, Houthi fighters, along with former president Ali Abdullah Saleh and his loyal troops, rebelled against the official Yemeni authorities represented by President Abdrabbuh Mansur Hadi. The rebels first occupied the state buildings in the capital Sanaa, before advancing into other cities – some of which they were able to capture – leading to a semi-civil conflict breaking out in multiple cities across Yemen.

soldiers jam-packed on the back, some of them grinning stupidly at the Peugeot drivers beside them. And finally, the military police cars. They escorted the army on its way to the south of the country.

I reached Aden in the second week of March. The missiles shook the city from all sides. Houthi militia bombed the Presidential Palace[2] in Maashiq. Army tanks trundled down the main streets. For the residents of Aden, the gunfire brought back bitter memories from the war of the summer of 1994;[3] they had no idea that a new, much bloodier one awaited them. On 23 March 2015, the decision to go to war was made; diplomats and international employees left Sanaa, while foreign embassies closed their doors and evacuated their personnel. Likewise, political party leaders departed the country with their families. I bade farewell to some of them in good faith. It didn't occur to me that they – having sensed the war was coming – decided to flee and leave us to our fate.

At that time, I was convinced the so-called civilized world wouldn't leave us to the foolishness of politicians and generals, that this world wouldn't just stand by idly watching us in the impending wreckage. That somebody would inevitably intervene – tomorrow, or maybe the day after, and stop us from wandering like an unknowing flock of sheep off a cliff. At 2 a.m. Thursday, 26 March,

2   The Presidential Palace that the Yemeni president Abdrabbuh Mansur Hadi resided in, in the southern Yemeni port Aden, after having fled the capital of Sanaa. He declared Aden the temporary capital.

3   On 27 April 1994, Ali Abdullah Saleh (president of unified Yemen from 1990 to 2012, assassinated by Houthi rebels 4 December 2017) declared war on his partner in the unified government, Ali Salem al-Beidh (the last president of the People's Democratic Republic of Yemen, or South Yemen). Saleh's armies stormed South Yemen. In 1990, the two presidents had agreed to unify the two countries.

when the Arab Coalition's[4] fighter planes suddenly cut through the Sanaa sky, war became a reality. From that morning, what's engraved on my mind isn't the roar of the explosions, or the horrifying thunder of planes piercing the sound barrier, nor my anxiety over the trajectory of missiles hitting targets further than I could see, nor the sounds of war that I had grown accustomed to. Rather, it is the shock of how war was conjured, how life collapsed in one fell swoop: civil infighting, the humiliation of hunger, the indignity of it all, our generation's lost dreams. They split the citizens into two warring camps, leaving the majority of us transformed into victims or voiceless beings.

—

I'm not concerned with listing the political details of the war here; instead, I have recorded in the introduction to this book the memories remaining in my mind of the bitter war we are still living through. An attempt to capture the essence of it all: the images of war I've seen and experienced, the disappearance of any kind of normal life, the damage and defeat that took root in my soul when the godfathers of war trampled patriotism, sovereignty and national unity beneath their heavy boots. But how can life in the shadow of a war that has destroyed everything

4   A military coalition created by Saudi Arabia to defend Yemen's official government represented by President Abdrabbuh Mansur Hadi against the Houthi and Saleh uprising. The Arab Coalition consists of ten countries: Saudi Arabia, the UAE, Bahrain, Kuwait, Morocco, Pakistan, Sudan, Egypt, Jordan and Qatar. Qatar excluded itself from the Arab Coalition in June 2017.

Translator's note: in 2019, Morocco and Sudan suspended their participation in the military coalition.

be fully encapsulated? What's undeniable is that we have returned to pre-civilization: all cities are without electricity, and we are living by the candlelight and gas lanterns used by our ancestors. And when the gas runs out at home, families resort to cutting down trees to use in wood stoves. There's no clean water to drink, so it has become a daily occurrence to witness children and the elderly queuing up with empty pots to fill from tankers donated by some good doer. Poverty can be seen wherever you turn: citizens have lost their jobs and livelihoods,[5] impoverished to the point they don't even question the meaning of war, it has devastated them so. Women and children fighting over scraps from rubbish piles, families sleeping outside, people displaced in miserable camps on the outskirts of cities, abandoned by the world and left forgotten there. Citizens have been stripped of their civil rights, blockaded by warring parties and countries that have taken military action in Yemen. When the Arab Coalition closed off the sea ports, land routes and national air space, thousands of citizens were stranded abroad. When the Arab Coalition finally reopened Aden International Airport, the blockade was still intact. No plane could take off from Yemeni airspace without permission from the leadership of the Arab Coalition. Friends shared the utter humiliation they endured at Bisha[6] airport. Police

5   On 18 September 2016, the Yemeni president Abdrabbuh
      Mansur Hadi issued the decision to move the central bank from
      the capital Sanaa, which had been captured by rebel forces,
      to Aden. The decision exacerbated the humanitarian crisis in
      Yemen as from its new location in Aden, the central bank failed
      to pay civil servants their salaries in Houthi-controlled areas.
      The rebel forces in Sanaa also refused to pay civil servants in the
      areas under their own control.
6   A Saudi Arabian airport located in Bisha, southwest of Saudi
      Arabia. Throughout the war, the airport was used to inspect
      those travelling on Yemeni civil aviation.

dogs sniffed their luggage as if they were criminals – yet another country violating their rights. The Arab Coalition even shut Sanaa airport in August 2016, further exacerbating the situation.

In the midst of this complete misery in which we are living, a different world has emerged: one of new villas whose cement boundary walls span several streets, lavish high-rises glittering in dusty backstreets, sprawling malls, new petrol stations, currency exchanges, private schools[7] and hospitals – all financed by stolen national revenue. This is the world of the new war rich, the war profiteers, the black-market tycoons, the relatives of the Houthi militia and of ex-president Ali Abdullah Saleh. The glamorous world of war has expanded, spreading to other capitals without us even knowing. The ministers, ambassadors and agents of the official Yemeni government waved the business flag of war from abroad. Elites who enrich themselves at the expense of the millions starving in Yemen. This is precisely why they, along with those they are fighting, are so keen for this war to last as long as possible.

They all live in a different time. A time outside the one where every day people are killed by air raids, missiles and mines. Where people are dying in prison cells, where people are made to disappear, their executioners leaving no trace. Where people are dying from hunger, cholera,[8] or some other plague. Where the war robs people of their

7   The warring parties privatized the government sector. Government schools have had funding cut, with teacher salaries not being paid. Government school fees were increased, and at the same time private schools were opened. The health and energy sectors were also privatized.

8   According to the World Health Organisation (WHO) report from 24 September 2017, 2,117 Yemenis died of cholera in the span of just five months.

15

dreams. And our lives carry on in this time, ruled by invisible forces, whose laws only apply to the likes of us. It is only we who have to face the absurdity of this war, only ordinary people who are paying the price.

I remember April during the first year of the war. The war was fresh in the city streets, shops were closed, and petrol stations out of service with lines of parked cars in front. It was four in the afternoon when my husband and I made our way to Dh'Amran Centre. Fighter planes dropped bombs over different areas in Sanaa. Though it was close by, I paid no attention to the roar of the explosions. But when the clouds of smoke veiled Attan mountain and Dh'Amran Centre, I suddenly felt in my bones the meaning of war. Moments like these happened again and again: planes bombing, militia firing missiles... But I remember that day at Mount Attan because my friend Mohammed al-Yemeni, who had been taking photos of the explosions that day, wrote to me saying, 'Why on earth did you come to Attan? You could have been killed!' Mohammed was himself killed a few months later by militia gunfire. In the wake of his death daily questions abound about this absurd war that spills the blood of innocents. Around me the list of the dead grows longer and longer: family, relatives, friends, neighbours – all civilians killed for no reason.

—

I write now by candlelight, no different from the beginning of the war. The roar of explosions swells, our windows shudder, the qamariyya cracks. We have only just repaired that crescent-shaped window after it shattered in the previous Coalition air raid. And so these explosions that rob people of their sleep, and sometimes of their lives, have become the backdrop to my writing about victims of war. It is as if time has stood still since I began writing and recording the testimonies of victims' families. I cannot forget the smell of charred human flesh, of singed hair stuck to the dusty factory floor after the Arab Coalition air raid on the al-Aqel factory in Sanaa.

In Taiz, my hometown, the situation is even more dire: the Houthi militia have imposed a blockade on the southern Yemeni city. I was forced to take a convoluted route. First, I had to drive round the entire city, then pass over mountains and through villages in the surrounding countryside, before finally arriving in Taiz. Even as we entered the city, the noise of the fighting between the Houthi-Saleh militia and pro-government resistance was unmistakable. You can't escape the scenes of destruction: homes destroyed, families forced to live in tents after the militia drove them out of their villages, despair in the eyes of citizens that sought refuge in the steep mountain passes such as Taluq[9] to find relief from the blockade. In the streets downtown, I encountered armed men belonging to the resistance, fighting one another. Stray bullets kill innocents every day. In the midst of this misery are the victims who have been ignored by those in power.

Visiting al-Hudaydah is extremely dangerous, as the militia are on the hunt for any journalists coming from outside the city. I went with my friend and made sure to wear the face covering traditional for Yemeni women. I arrived just as the people were anxiously waiting for the Arab Coalition forces to enter the city. The hospitals were overwhelmed with civilian air raid victims. I saw with my own eyes what a spider bomb did to the body of

9   A mountain pass located on Mount Sabr. The inhabitants of
     Taiz used it to transport oxygen to their hospitals and transfer
     foodstuffs.

a poor fishmonger. Bones protruded from bodies defeated by hunger. I saw fear in the eyes of those who didn't know what had happened to their loved ones, dozens of whom died under torture. Al-Hudaydah is no exception in this giant prison called Yemen, but it is the place where suffering caused by arbitrary arrests and disappearances has been greatest. In Taiz, to the southwest, schools have become prisons where innocent people[10] vanish, never to return. In the southern cities, with multiple powers fighting for leadership, funded by Saudi Arabia, Iran, and the Emirates, prisoners also die in captivity.[11]

There is so much to say about this nation that no longer belongs to us but rather to those engaged in war, so many details reinforced by the bitterness of conflict. When a group of armed men from the Southern Resistance stopped us near the city of al-Dhalea', I experienced first-hand what it means to be a stranger in your own country. For the simple reason that we had come from the north, they didn't allow us to continue on our journey until they received the official say-so from the Emirati troops. In Aden, a secondary war has broken out over who will control the city. It is being waged by local militia with the help of the 'liberators' (Saudi Arabia and the Emirates). Armed men of the South Yemeni separatist movement are fighting against the troops of the presidential guard, while the United Arab Emirates Air Force bombs Aden

10 This is what happened in the case of the political activist Ayyub al-Salihi, who disappeared on 29 June 2016, and whose whereabouts are still unknown. Armed factions affiliated with the Islah party, also known as the Yemeni Congregation for Reform, are suspected.
11 According to a 22 June 2017 Human Rights Watch report, the United Arab Emirates is said to be responsible for managing some of the prisons in southern Yemen and to be involved in the torture of detainees.

International Airport. I realized in this particular moment of history how absolutely symmetrical and similar opponents can be.

—

Only victims are real in this war, victims crushed by violence. The war has entered its fourth year, and the death toll is in the tens of thousands. It has destroyed the nation and divided the people. And yet, this war seems to raise few moral questions among most intellectuals in the country. Hardly any seem to wonder what this war actually means for all of us. What it means for planes from other countries to bomb our cities. What it means for innocent people to be killed. Sometimes I explain away the lack of conscience among our cultural elite as a result of being terrorized by those in charge of the war. But the more I think about it, the more I realize that these intellectuals, media professionals, journalists and human rights activists have contributed to the terror by taking one side or the other, and are in fact supporting the war. Some of them were even my friends. In times of peace, we shared our dreams with each other, which were one and the same. But now they have denounced us, turned their generals against us, sometimes becoming bloodthirsty hunting dogs themselves. They track down our writings, betray us and make killing us permissible.

The hunting dogs began to bark when any of the Yemeni intelligentsia spoke out against the war, against the murder of innocent people, against how they impoverished and left us broken, against the cost they imposed on our future generations.

Those who had signed an appeal to all the warring parties to make peace were persecuted and denounced as traitors. The Houthi-leaning *al-Hawya* newspaper, headed by Mohammed Ali al-Emad, published the names of the signatories under the headline: 'The Ninth Column: Agents and Mercenaries of the Saudi Aggression.' In addition, the newspapers[12] affiliated to and financed by the militia defamed all journalists who took a stand against the war. Journalist Nabeel Sabee[13] was shot and journalist Mohammed al-Abasi was murdered.[14] Yahya al-Jabihi was also sentenced to death by a Houthi court on charges of 'communicating with the enemy'.[15] But hunting dogs and witch hunts aren't only for the militia-owned media. Pro-government journalists, human rights activists and media professionals target anyone who condemns the murder of civilians by the Saudi-led Coalition, criticizes the corruption of the government, or even calls for peace. Accusations were made that writers were guilty of being neutral or belonging to the 'soft network of the coup'. The anchors of the Belqees channel[16] were at the head of this smear campaign.

In one of the interviews with an activist on this channel, the anchor accused him of supporting the militia in Taiz. Armed men from the pro-government resistance

12 Such as *al-Thawra* newspaper that was seized by the militia, and the newspaper *La* that is headed by the journalist Sallah al-Dakkak, a Houthi supporter.
13 Nabeel Sabee, a Yemeni poet and journalist who was nearly assassinated on 2 January 2016 in Sanaa.
14 Mohammed al-Abasi (1980–2016), a Yemeni investigative journalist who wrote a number of reports on the oil deals and corruption within the Houthi movement. He was threatened, then poisoned on 20 December 2016.
15 On 13 April 2017, the Criminal Court issued Yahya al-Jabihi with a death sentence. However, a year after his abduction and imprisonment, he was released. His son Hamza remains in captivity.
16 The Belqees news channel is owned by Nobel Peace Prize laureate, Tawakkol Karman, and supported by Qatar.

were soon surrounding his home.[17] The dark irony of it all is that the agitators are always either beneficiaries of the respective military powers on the inside, or reside in Arab or European capitals, far from the war raging in their own country. And still, from that distance they decide who deserves to call themselves a patriot among those remaining in Yemen, those left to weather the storms that almost uproot them.

—

Another explosion. The candle is melting and will soon die out. But it will leave a trace on the table, to remind me that something once burnt here. The scars of war don't go away. They stay in our souls, and in our memory. They remain alive in the minds of all those who have experienced war and suffered its destruction, all of those who have lost their loved ones. The horrors of this war and our tragedy cannot be forgotten, simply because the world wants to pull the curtain down over it, to hide the victims and to reward the executioners. So, then, these witness testimonies, their voices are a finger in the eyes of the murderers and the hunting dogs whom they hide behind. They are a testament to ward against forgetting, against feigning ignorance, against indifference. They are a balm for the souls of all those who have been killed, those whose loved ones have been left behind, left with nothing but memories.

Bushra al-Maqtari
March 2018, Sanaa

17 On 28 May 2017, troops of the resistance surrounded Abdel
    Salam al-Shumari's home in Taiz, forcing him to flee the city.
    This was after the interview with anchor Aswan Shahir on
    Belqees channel, where she accused him of supporting the coup.

It had to be a horror film; it was unreal. A film with no sound or actors. One that directed itself, only about a second long, and that only I saw that day: missiles flying, arriving from the west, falling, then hitting my brother's house. I always pause at that moment, playing it over in my head, at times speeding it up to see for myself what happened afterwards and at others pausing it, then letting it play in slow motion until the details are etched in my memory. I interfere in the film, freezing the missiles and pausing time itself, again and again. The nights when I see my brother sad and silent, and my attempts to console him are of no avail, I imagine what if I'd had the power to stop those missiles, or if the universe had stepped in at that very moment with an earthquake or a hurricane, something bigger than us all, making those missiles explode mid-air before they had the chance to destroy our lives. But now I think of how missiles don't just fall from the sky, there's a mind behind them, a villain who presses the button to lock in a target: my brother's home, killing women and children.

Look around you. There's nothing here in al-Qutay,[18] nothing, [*he falls silent*] just scattered homes of poor families, a repair garage, a marketplace. No military barracks, patrols, militia, or even armed men. For years it's only been us living here, we've had nothing to do with the war going on, trying to live in peace, but then they came here with their missiles and killed my brother's family. [*He takes out a cigarette and smokes.*] Some days later I heard what some people were saying and lost it. They were saying that the Coalition's missiles had targeted the aerial of

18 A town that falls under the administration of the Marawiah
    district in the al-Hudaydah governorate.

SabaFon Mobile Company next to my brother's house. Liars. Bastards. If what they were saying was true then the Coalition should have warned the residents: 'Listen up you fools, we're going to blow up this damn useless aerial.' We would have then immediately picked up our children and run away with our families to the desert. But the aerial wasn't touched, instead the missile fell on my brother's house, which had been the target all along.

I don't know what made me stop at that moment. In the film in my head, I don't stop, but what actually happened was different. Fear seized my body when I saw death before my eyes, I froze, and thought of what was going to happen. My brother was next to me but looking in another direction, I don't know where I got the strength from. I held Fahmi tight in my arms, so that he wouldn't see, but when he turned round, he saw the explosion and the smoke rising from his house. He struggled against me, I hugged him tighter and let him cry, his body shaking in my arms. Some friends came and helped me stabilize him. 'Keep an eye on him, I'll go and have a look.' I was afraid that he'd hurt himself. [*He cries and puts out his cigarette.*]

I was the first to go into the house, alone; I didn't think about the roof, which could have fallen in at any moment. What I saw was horrific, I couldn't get any closer – I stood where I was, in the middle of it all, not aware of what was around me. After some time, a few families arrived together, carrying away pieces of furniture and other things. They were ransacking the house. I couldn't stop them, I was numb. [*He cries.*]

I didn't pay attention to Fahmi, I was staring at the burnt bodies, the crushed bodies, the dismembered bodies, the distorted bodies, some of which had been flung outside the house because the blast had been so powerful. First, I saw some women neighbours and a child from our area, and then on the opposite side, my sister-in-law, her young son Mohammed, and her two daughters Malak and Malakat. When I saw Malakat dead, her hands and feet missing, my tears started to fall. Oh Malakat! Oh darling, I wish I had taken you with me. That day she wouldn't leave my side, she had asked, 'Ammu, take me with you.' I carried her with me and took her out to the shop, then dropped her back home. Minutes later, the missile hit. [*He cries bitterly.*]

My brother's screams that day, the missile whistling in the air, then falling on his house, the smoke, the burnt bodies. These are the images and the sounds that have kept me awake for months. Sometimes I dream of the moment just before the missile fell, and in those dreams, I always manage to stop it.

My brother is still tormented, he can't sleep, he can't forget. He's preoccupied with finding treatment for his injured son. I carry my brother's sorrows on my back, I enter the house and the memories come rushing back. I remember my brother's children and his wife, their laughter, the noise they would make, our beautiful life together. Damn the Coalition and whoever came with them to our country, damn every side that has murdered Yemeni people. They're all just that – murderers. Who will bring back Malak, Malakat, Mohammed and Asma to my brother? Who? Tell me who? Who?

No one. No one cares about what happened to us.

Ahmad Abdel Hameed Sayf

At 5.40 p.m. on Thursday, 26 January 2017, the Arab Coalition aeroplanes targeted Ahmad's brother's house, Fahmi Abdel Hameed Sayf in al-Qutay in the governorate of al-Hudaydah. His brother's wife Asma Abdel Qader Yassin Sharaf

25

(30 years old) was killed, and her children: Mohammed Fahmi Abdel Hameed Sayf (12 years old), Malak Fahmi Abdel Hameed Sayf, (3 years old), Malakat Fahmi Abdel Hameed Sayf (18 months), as well as another girl Nisreen Hassan Zayd Mohammed (10 years old), and three women and two children from their neighbour Abdel Kareem Abdel Hameed's family. Ammar Fahmi Abdel Hameed Sayf (8 years old) was injured and his left leg amputated. He is now disabled and no one is helping with his treatment. SabaFon Mobile Company refused to compensate the families or pay towards any treatment.

Cold, dust and wind slip into our house through the skeletons of the qamariyya stained-glass crescents and the empty window frames. Rain finds its way in too; we can't protect ourselves from the cold. My husband repairs the glass once more, but with every militia bomb it shatters over our heads. I finally convinced my husband to just let them be, and I'm happy with that. Reem is there, I feel her in the air I breathe. Whenever the cold afternoon breeze blows, I feel her spirit in the air; it stays in my bones, reminding me that I lost my daughter in the war.

Our grandmothers say that when children die, they go to heaven, and become angels. I always think of Reem as a tiny angel with rose wings flying around up above us: dancing, laughing, singing along with other children who were killed by life or by war. But children who die in war leave sorrow behind in their mothers' hearts, and my sorrow eats me alive. I remember that day. It's a pain that won't go away; sometimes I'm attacked by the exhausting feeling that I'm the reason she died. Other times I move on from the torment and convince myself that it was an absurd coincidence, or fate. It just so happened that Reem, her sister Malak, and other children from the neighbourhood were in front of the shop when the shell hit. The killers, they're the ones responsible for this tragedy, for our pain; but guilt will always gnaw away at a mother – a mother who spent her life protecting her children, a mother who let her two children go out and die.

I remember Reem all the time: playing with her sisters Malak and Bushra, their brother Malek annoying them. Her imitating her grandmother Hajja. If her gedda started praying then Reem would also take out her mat and pray next to her, or if her gedda lay down, Reem did the very same thing. In such moments I'm far away from the noise of the world and the roar of the bombing, I'm protected from the horror that fills the streets of Bir Basha, the district where the war doesn't take a breath, not even for a moment.

At the beginning of the war, we were forced to move to the Maqbana district and stay in the village for two months. But as Hajja says, it felt more like two years of misery. No water, no electricity. In the mornings we would go to the distant mountain to gather firewood, our hands and feet raw. We couldn't stay there any longer and came back home. We patched up the broken windows, but after three days the shells hit our house. One fell on the roof and destroyed our water tanks. I counted my children. I didn't let them take a step outside.

I don't know why I told Reem and Malak to buy a packet of potato chips for their younger sister that day. I can still remember them both, going down the building stairs, Reem in her pink trousers and a smart jacket. I had cut her hair two days before; she had been sitting in front of the mirror looking at herself and smiling. [*She falls silent, shrinking into herself.*] The balcony door slamming is what pulled me out of my daydream, then smoke began to fill the room. My youngest daughter was crying; I picked her up and went down the stairs, my husband was standing there. 'Reem . . . she's with Allah.' I went into the alley. Blood was on the shop steps, potato chips mixed with blood, Reem, my baby, and other children, dead, headless. [*She cries.*] What did Reem do to deserve this? She was just a young girl, they kept her from me, they broke my heart.

Malak doesn't walk any more; the shrapnel pierced her body. Every day she recalls how she was holding her sister's hand while they were waiting for their friends Ruba and Rafaa, to play together. 'Mama, Reem didn't have a face,' she tells me. 'The bomb wiped away my sister's face.'

In Malak's nightmares I hear the shell as it falls a thousand times. Then, my daughter and the other children, without heads. Malak recounts the terrible details over and over, sweating in her sleep, talking about her sister's head in pieces on the fourth step of the shop. I hug her and cry, and that's when the cold gusts of wind slip in, and I think of Reem, hovering above us with her tiny angel wings.

Nussaibah Abdel Malek

At 4.15 p.m. on Monday, 3 October 2016, the Houthi and Ali Abdullah Saleh militia targeted a shop in the Bir Basha district in the city of Taiz. The following were killed: Reem Bashir (4 years old, Nussaibah's daughter), Saeed Mohammed Saeed (10 years old), Mohammed Fawwaz Mohammed (10 years old), Bashar Mohammed Qaid (11 years old), Ali Abdu Saeed (9 years old), Mujed Nasser Saeed (28 years old), Mohammed Abdullah Abdu (20 years old), Haytham Qaid Mansour (20 years old), Ismail Mohammed Ahmad (35 years old), and Aseel Mahyub Ghalib (17 years old). Malak Bashir (Nussaibah's other daughter, 8 years old) was injured.

I'll never forget them; I dream about them all the time. I get lost in their voices, their chatter, their laughter. Their lives are right here beside me, they're with me everywhere I go: the house, the farm, the market... When I wake up and they're not there, I remember that they are in the bowels of the earth, protected. I carry my son's and grandchildren's photos in my wallet, I look at them and tell them about how dry life has become without them, about the rain that never fell, about the fruit of the mango tree that they will never taste. I tell them how weary I am without them here, the pain in my joints, my chest infection, about my wife sick with grief, who thinks of them and cries. Only God knows what's in my heart. Whom should I complain to? I'm unwell; the way my heart aches for my son and grandchildren will be the end of me. [*He looks at what remains of his son's house.*] Husni was my youngest son, he was thirty years old when they killed him; Qabul, his wife, was twenty-five; Taqiya, my granddaughter, was just ten years old, she was in the fifth grade; Fatima was eight years old, she was in the third grade; Sara was five years old; and Mohammed was two. Where are they now? Where am I? They killed them in their sleep; why? They were innocent. There's nothing to bomb here, just some farmers trying to make a living – who would do such a thing? Who could be this barbaric? [*He falls silent, looking off in the direction of his son's home.*]

Thinking of that early morning makes my chest hurt; I don't know where I am, why I'm still alive. [*He cries.*] It was three-thirty in the morning, all you could hear on the farm were the crickets chirping. My whole family was asleep. Our houses are right next to each other's. There's mine, my brother's, my eldest son's and then Husni's.

Only a few metres separate my house from his. I was half asleep, tossing in my bed. I prayed the dawn prayer and was slipping back into sleep when I heard the first missile, BOOM. Judgement Day had come. I jumped out of bed like a madman, I hadn't heard anything like it since the start of the war. I ran to the farm to see what'd happened. My brother had escaped from his house with his family, finding shelter somewhere else on the farm. I ran towards the sound, thinking that the blast had taken place further away, and that the silence and the calmness of the wind had exaggerated the sound, carrying it from the location of the explosion. There was nothing in this area for them to bomb. I took off in another direction, not able to see anything in the dark. Afterwards I realized I needed to warn Husni to get his family out of the house, and while I was running, the second missile hit, then the third, then the fourth – four missiles altogether, five minutes between each one, falling next to my son's house. [*He stops, his mind elsewhere.*]

I ran to Husni's house. [*He pauses.*] It was over. The house had collapsed on my son and grandchildren. The force of the missile threw my son's body ten metres into the field. We found his hand next to this well, his wife and children's bodies next to that tree. Everyone from the village rushed here, they moved my family's limbs from in front of me while I watched their footsteps that dawn, disbelieving. [*His voice wavers, he chokes on his tears.*] How would we get them to the hospital? There was nothing to save. For hours, the villagers gathered their limbs, sticking the parts back together. We waited for the sun to rise and buried them in the cemetery here.

Right where you're standing, that's where we found Husni's body. [*He looks intently at the rocks that were once a house, as if trying to awaken the dead, speaking to them.*]

Husni was my youngest, the apple of my eye. He would provide for us, me and his mother, he was our pillar. Losing him, I lost everything. I only have one son now. Every day I ask myself: why did they kill them? What did my son and grandchildren do to deserve this? They killed my son, his wife, my four grandchildren at dawn, while they were sleeping. Who would do such a thing?

[*I fall silent, having no words to soothe the anguish of this eighty-something-year-old man.*

He looks at what was left of his son's house, and tries to mask his despair. The rocks are the only sign that a house once stood here. The sound of the pump, used by the people of Deir al-Hajari, grows louder. The old man's gaze falls on the rubble. He points to his son's family's belongings in a heap next to the stones: red torn rugs, burnt blankets, children's clothes bleached by the sun, a bed, now a heap of twisted metal.]

This is where Husni's house was. There's his bedroom, his children's room, that is where we used to sit together. Where are they now, and where am I? At every moment, I raise my hands to the sky and curse the Coalition. I curse those who killed my son and his family, and those who are behind all the death and devastation in this country.

Ali Ahmad Jaber al-Ahdal

At 3.30 a.m. on Saturday, 8 October 2016, the Arab Coalition planes targeted his son Husni's home in Deir al-Hajari, a village in the Bajil district in the governorate of al-Hudaydah. His son, Husni Ali Ahmad Jaber al-Ahdal (30 years old), was killed, as well as his daughter-in-law, Qabul Mohammed Hussein (27 years old), and their daughters: Taqiya Husni Ali Ahmad Jaber al-Ahdal (10 years old), Fatima Husni Ali Ahmad Jaber al-Ahdal (8 years old), Sarah Husni Ali Ahmad Jaber al-Ahdal (5 years old), and their son Mohammed Husni

Ali Ahmad Jaber al-Ahdal (2 years old). The grandfather Ali Ahmad Jaber al-Ahdal's house was destroyed. No one helped him except for UNICEF, which donated some wood to build a shed to protect him and his wife from the elements.

A STORY THAT MUST BE PUT TO BED

A week ago I was blessed with a boy; I named him Usaid [*she bites her nails anxiously*], after my firstborn who was killed. I wish I didn't remember what happened. I – my husband and I – try to forget. In the early days, we would remember our children and cry – then, after some time we would each grieve alone. When Mohammed's mind wanders and his eyes glaze over, black, I know very well in those moments he's missing them. He doesn't talk about the children, and when I ask him about them, he goes quiet. I cry, and he becomes sad and withdrawn. I have now convinced myself to not mention the children in front of him. I leave my sadness inside, lock it up in my heart. With time, a pain has grown between us, one that occupies a giant space in our lives. Even so, I haven't wanted to make life harder for him, he has struggled so hard to forget. What happened is still there in his injured eye, his glass eye that contains it all. [*I told her that when I'd interviewed her husband, he'd collapsed crying, so I stopped recording.*]

Each of us has tried to keep our grief to ourselves, so as not to reopen the other's wounds. After *it* happened, we were displaced. Throughout the year, we moved from one house to another, and when we returned to our neighbourhood, the memories rose up once more. I remember my children all the time and cry. I didn't want to come back here, but I agreed because this is where my husband's shop is. We rented this place after our home attached to the shop was destroyed. But everything in this neighbourhood reminds me of them: life, the sounds, the children's laughter. [*She bites her nails and grows silent.*]

Whenever someone visited me, I'd start wailing uncontrollably, not knowing who I was any more. The thing is, I don't have the kind of mind that can forget. I stay silent; Mohammed grows sadder. When we hear the bombs, I say, 'The shells will kill us this time.' But when they pass over us, I think of the house that those shells destroyed, I think of corpses, dead children, grieving mothers. That's when I wish we lived in a room underground, so I wouldn't hear the bombs or the news of death.

I lost my baby in the first months of the war, when I was still in my first month of pregnancy. My children were killed after. [*She cries.*] But what makes my story special? It's the same for the many thousands of women who have lost their children to war. In every house in this city, there's a story that must be put to bed, one that no one should reawaken. [*She looks off into the distance.*] I'm tired. I've been in this room overlooking the alleys the whole time, and from this low window, I've been able to hear the children's squeals and shouting, my children's friends playing, carrying on as if nothing has changed. Life goes on around me, indifferent to me, I, a mother whose children were taken by war with nothing left but her memories of them.

I remember my son Usaid and my daughter Rahma playing in the neighbourhood, while I tidied up the house and prepared lunch. They raised their voices so that I could make sure they were nearby. Such things would comfort me. But what's the use of remembering now?

When I think of them being killed, I fall apart. [*She cries.*] I remember my last words with my uncle, I was standing in the basement room we used to live in, my children playing around me like always; I was reassured by their racket. My uncle picked up my son Ezzedine and said, 'I'll take him with me outside to get some fresh air.' I didn't think that would be the last time I'd ever see them. [*She cries.*]

I felt a tightness in my chest, I couldn't breathe, and asked myself, 'Why is the basement so hot today? Why is it so dark, even though the lights are on?' As Mohammed was getting ready to go out, he said, 'The resistance has freed the al-Qahira Castle! The world is safe again, let the children play outside.' Hearing what her father said, Rahma took her twin sister and went out, with the others following behind. I don't know why I let them go out. [*She weeps bitterly.*]

The basement walls crumbled under the force of the blast, the world around me grew dark. I called out to Mohammed to bring the children inside, but he didn't answer. Then I heard a scream, like the sound of an animal being slaughtered; it was Mohammed. The world began to spin. I ran outside into the street. [*She cries and bites her nails. She fans her fingers out and looks at them.*] I called out to my husband again, not paying attention to the blood flowing from his eye. Looking at the corpses, he grew pale and fainted. I ran around the courtyard screaming and screaming, seeing my children's bodies. [*She cries.*] Blood covered my uncle's face, but he was still breathing, choking out his words. He pointed to my children. I didn't understand what he was saying, I was running from one edge of the courtyard to another, then I stopped. When my eyes landed on my son Usaid and his brother Ezzedine, I lost all control. They told me afterwards that Usaid had been playing the helicopter game with him, carrying his brother in the air to make him fly when the missile hit them both.

My children – Usaid, Ezzedine, and Rahma – were laid out next to their grandfather. I only saw my children. I couldn't even hear the voices of those injured around me, seeking help. I stood next to my children, Usaid was lying lifeless, Rahma had a huge gash in her back. Seeing them like that, I had no control over myself. I was screaming, crying, and no one answered me. An elderly man carried Ezzedine in front of me. I couldn't look at him. My other daughter Mawadda was injured, she had been with her twin Rahma when the missile hit. Her sister flew through the air right before her eyes. The people in the neighbourhood told me that my children were fine, and that Usaid was still alive. They also said that Rahma had survived, but I didn't believe them. I remember her body, ripped open, and knew that she had left this world. But maybe Ezzedine...I still held out hope. I didn't find out that he hadn't survived until the next morning, when I left the house and saw men and women around the ambulance, and a man showed me his body. I couldn't touch him. [*She cries.*]

My daughter Mawadda is still in shock, she has lost her twin, her lifelong playmate. She was pierced by shrapnel and still hasn't got any better, always in her own world; when she sees a stranger in our house, she hides. She doesn't want her sister's name to be said in her presence, and when she plays with the neighbourhood children, she avoids anyone who mentions Rahma. She refuses to go to the school where she had studied with her sister. The one day she went, she came home in tears.

I visit my children in the cemetery whenever I get the chance, but I'm still not convinced that they're dead. Living in memories is painful because you realize that no matter what you do, they've become just that, a memory, no longer a real life. My husband hid their photos, he doesn't want me to see them because I'll cry, and that will be the end of him. But I was able to get some from a friend, and have stored them away.

I'll never forget my children. Every day I curse the militia, they've robbed me of my children and now I only see them in my dreams. I don't want anyone to visit me. I just want to cry alone.

Sumaiyya Ahmad Saeed

At 4.30 p.m. on Friday, 20 August 2015, the Houthi-Saleh militia targeted a group of children next to the shop belonging to her husband, Mohammed Qasim Rashid al-Khadami, in al-Dhabou'a neighbourhood in the city of Taiz. Three of her children were killed: Usaid Mohammed Qasim Rashid al-Khadami (8 years old), Rahma Mohammed Qasim Rashid al-Khadami (6 years old), Ezzedine Mohammed Qasim Rashid al-Khadami (2 years old), and her father-in-law, Ahmad Ali Ahmad al-Khadami (50 years old), as well as other children from the neighbourhood.

My sister says that my children's murder turned me into someone else. Sometimes, when I look at myself a year on, I believe her, and when I remember how I was that day, I realize steadfastness has protected my heart. But don't believe it when people say that faith and patience come just like that; they need practice. After my house crashed down on their heads that day, I was grieving my children. It's true that I refused to see them – I wanted to remember them as they were: beautiful, joyful, loving. [*She falls silent.*]

It was just like any other day, except my daughter's friends were over. I remember how happy she was to have them there; she hadn't seen them for months. I looked intently at her radiant face, a mother mesmerized by her only daughter, who was shortly to be engaged. Two days earlier, her aunt had asked for Noura's hand for her son. 'I'll think about it,' Noura had said. That day, I wanted to give her and her friends some privacy. I told Noura, 'I'm going over to Um Lubna's, make sure to call Shuhab inside if it looks like rain.' At 4.15 p.m., I heard the planes overhead and told myself, 'Maybe they'll bomb Jabal Nuqum[19] or Erat Hamdan,[20] as they did during the war.' In that moment I remembered my son Shuhab, and how scared he'd get by the sound of the planes. Whenever he heard them, he'd yank on my neck to shield him, and I'd get impatient saying, 'You're choking me, Shuhab, you're choking me, Ibni.' In his trembling voice he'd respond, 'Mama, I'm holding you tight so you don't get scared.' My neighbour Um Lubna told me, 'Don't worry, Shuhab's probably inside now.' The windows exploded and shards

19 A mountain located to the east of Sanaa.
20 al-Erat village, the highest point in the vicinity, which falls under the Hamdan district of the Sanaa governorate.

of glass flew around us. Um Lubna's house filled with smoke. 'I'll have a look outside,' her sister said, 'and check on Shuhab...Khala, your house isn't there.' [*She falls silent.*]

Can you imagine? Your house and everyone in it, just gone, swallowed whole by the earth. When I saw the remains of my house through their window frame, I was unable to speak. I don't remember how I held myself together, how I crossed the few metres to where the house had been, replaced now by a hole six metres deep. All I remember are the limbs on the ground, the plane circling above our heads, the smoke everywhere, and me, in shock, staring at what was left of my home, and of my neighbour's which had been partly destroyed.

Faces streamed past me. Limbs, corpses. My son Khalid was digging to get his siblings out. He held up a small foot and my legs gave way. It was Shuhab's leg, it definitely was. This wasn't simply a mother's intuition; I recognized the black trousers and jacket I'd dressed him in that morning. In a fog, I made out the neighbours searching for what was left of their loved ones; I was far away from them, in another world, my mind blank. Rain washed over my head and eyes; all I saw were bodies digging, digging and digging to unearth a man, or the hand of a son or daughter. I walked aimlessly, leaving behind what had been our home – one of the neighbourhood women saw me and took me to a clinic nearby. The clinic was full of injured people. I saw my other neighbour; they had pulled her from the rubble. She was mourning her four children who had been killed. I held her in my arms and repeated to myself the truth of what happened. She was rambling her children's names, and then she screamed, 'They killed Shuhab, they killed Noura!' I left the clinic knowing I would never see them again.

Unlike the perpetrator, they say a victim never returns

to the scene of the crime, but I did. Something pulled me back. My brother tried to take me to his house instead. 'I just want to go home,' I said through my tears. I knew my house was no longer there, it would only stand now in my memories. In an instant my home was wiped off the map, and my two children Shuhab and Noura, as well as Noura's friends, killed. With the power of steadfast faith or perhaps sheer disbelief, I stood staring at the hole. I didn't yell like other mothers who've lost their children, I didn't strike my face in lament; I refused to look at my children's limbs. I stood silent that day among the rubble, looking at what was no longer there. Steadfastness took root in that moment, washing over me like cool water; in that moment when I sat in front of the remains of my home, where everything I had was gone, steadfastness forced me to face reality, to remember my daughter Noura as I had last seen her, laughing, happy with her friends, and Shuhab, playing, singing, unafraid of the plane that would kill him.

You have no idea how much steadfastness can give you when disaster strikes. Strength perhaps, maybe numbness, as my sister says. But I dream that one day I'll be with Noura and Shuhab, and that we'll be in another beautiful home. My neighbour, who lost four of her children, refuses to look at where our houses had once stood. Whenever she passes by what were our homes, she takes a detour. But I don't want to forget, I want to remember everything, beautiful as it was before this all happened – that's what gives me the endurance to carry on with the rest of my family. I'm not crazy like my sister claims. Three days after the bombing, I wanted to see what had once been my home, and convinced my sister to take me there. To her, this was madness, and she said I wasn't in my right mind. She cried, remembering how she used to come over from her place by the airport to our house, and how warmly Noura and Shuhab would welcome her. I didn't cry. I just stared at the hole that swallowed up my family, and lost myself in the memories of time past, sheltered by the home my husband had toiled years to build. A place to protect us from the elements, the home that was no longer, the home that was replaced by a pit.

In my mind, I look into the heart of the pit: I remember our life in the disappeared house, my daughter Noura, how happy she was, how cherished she was, how everyone loved her. Her whole life had been in front of her. I remember my son Shuhab playing in the hallways; I remember life as perfect and complete. Wordless, I go on looking and looking deep down into the hole. Nothing – no amount of crying or regret – can ever make up for the loss of my children.

Sabah Abda Ahmad Fare

At 5.30 p.m. on Tuesday, 2 June 2015, the Arab Coalition's planes targeted the home of Ali Ahmad Mohammed Al Qabali in Erat Hamdan in Sanaa. Sabah's daughter, Noura Ali Ahmad Mohammed Al Qabali (19 years old) was killed, along with her son Shuhab Ali Ahmad Mohammed Al Qabali (5 years old). Her daughter's friends were also killed: Lubna Sultan and Ishraq al-Zaifi. From her neighbour's family, Qaid al-Atmi, four children were killed: Rudaina al-Atmi, Ameera al-Atmi, Abdo al-Atmi, Adeeb al-Atmi. The Coalition destroyed Ali Ahmad Mohammed al-Qabali's house that he had built himself.

WE'LL BE RIGHT BACK, MAMA

Their laughter echoes through this empty house. I stretch out my hand, feeling the shadowy corners, stroking the frames bordering a dull emptiness. I touch their faces one by one; I clasp my hands...Aya, my daughter, laughs and runs from me. I follow her through the rooms and up the stairs, where she disappears. I hear her steps on the roof and shrink into myself, her laughter echoing from within the walls. Loudly, happily, she says, 'We'll be right back Mama, just a minute, and we'll be down,' 'Don't worry, Mama, we're coming down now.' Hand in hand, she and her younger sister, Raghad, are standing on the stairs, just like the last time I saw them. Girls, where are you? Aya? Where are you, Raghad? I run after their fading voices and laughter; silence and darkness return once more. I stare into the darkness and an invisible curtain opens in the ceiling – light floods the corners of every room, lively voices rush in, powerful and loud. My husband Abdulkareem smiles tenderly, like the last time I saw him. But then the light transforms into an abyss of choppy water, the water tossing him back and forth; he paddles with his bare hands, growing tired, on the verge of drowning. Aya grabs one of his hands and Raghad the other, dragging him to the shore. But I remember this is the dream my husband had a week before the girls were killed, before he soon followed. I wave, holding my son. 'Take me with you!' The voices and laughter disappear, and I'm back where I am now, staring at these blue walls. [*She cries bitterly and wails. She stands then sits down once more.*]

It was 14 August 2015, noon: the sun's rays shone through the windows overlooking the city's alleys, the neighbourhood children's voices came from far away, and

I couldn't make out their racket from the airstrikes in the suburbs. It was a Friday, the sound of the muezzin's call to prayer rising above the houses, spreading a peace that I had missed. My husband went to pray and I started preparing lunch; kebsa was on the fire, and I stirred it gently until it was well-cooked. I wasn't pulled in by the roar of the shells that fell on the city from time to time, I was stuck in the little world of my family – whom I lived for, and for whom I cut off all ties with the outside world – of my beloved husband, my two daughters and my two young sons. A few minutes and then we can eat, I thought.

My two daughters, Aya and Raghad, insisted on fetching water from the tank on the roof. 'Don't go up there,' I told them. 'Can't you hear the shelling?' 'We'll go real quick and come back with the water,' they said. Aya brought down a jug of water and told me, 'Mama, there's only two jugs left. We'll go up and be back before you know it.'

Both of them went up, their voices from the stairwell reassuring me, 'Don't worry, Mama, we'll be down in just a second. We'll be right back.' [*She chokes up and cries, distressed.*]

The force of the explosion extinguished the flame on the gas stove. Then I heard the deafening sound of the shell, the closest I'd heard one throughout the whole war. My son ran into the kitchen. I remembered my girls...how did I get to them? Did I run? Fly? Did my feet even carry me? I don't know. I remember when I got to the floor above, where my father-in-law's flat was, telling myself the girls would be there. They love playing with their cousins. I looked around. Where are Aya and Raghad? Everyone was stunned; they kept looking at me. I climbed the last steps to the roof. It was enveloped in silence, dust from the shelling and the smell of blood. It was just me, and my two daughters spread out on the floor; a pool of blood and silence. Aya's hand lay protectively on her sister, her feet a lump of flesh next to her. Her terrified eyes stared into mine. Raghad's face and body were covered in dust. I couldn't touch either of them, and just screamed and screamed. No one answered. [*She cries standing where she is, looking around, eyes glazed over.*]

When I opened my eyes, I grew aware of women crying, crowded around me. From then on, I survived on sedatives, in limbo between hope and reality. Seeing my husband keeping it together, I realized what bad shape I was in. Losing my daughters ripped out my heart. Just a few weeks later, I told my husband, 'I want a daughter, I want to get pregnant, I want to hold another life.' It worked; I grew pregnant, defying death with the being growing in my womb. [*She falls silent.*]

But war wasn't done with me yet. Three months after my daughters' murder, I was in this room, the house full of condoling women; I don't know what came over me that day. I grabbed my husband, and forbade him from going outside. 'Don't go out, Abdulkareem,' I pleaded. 'I have a bad feeling.' Whenever anyone went out, I thought it would be for the last time. In his warm manner, he comforted me, 'Don't worry, Munira. Calm down. You're exhausted.'

When the Asr call to prayer rang out, a child from my husband's side of the family ran in, crying. 'A bullet hit Abdulkareem! They shot Abdulkareem!'

The ICU doctor told me he would survive. Then I heard my uncle's voice; he was looking for me. 'It's Abdulkareem...I'm so sorry...Thank God you're still alive.' But who said I'm alive? I'm not alive, I'm dead now. They destroyed me, they took away everything beautiful in my life. I clung to my sons, and embraced the child in my belly, all I had left of my husband – but they even took that. A few weeks after my husband's murder, a grenade fell next to the house. I jumped up to protect my sons, and in the morning when I saw the blood, I knew I'd lost my son or daughter to be.

My uncle Mohammed al-Haddad would come to check on me every day. I'd wait for his arrival; it gave me hope. 'I won't leave you Munira,' he'd tell me, 'you're not alone. Nothing is going to happen to you while I'm around.' [*She cries.*] But they robbed me of that hope too – the militia targeted my uncle's house on Jamal Street and killed him. That day, everything inside me died. [*She cries bitterly.*] I don't know whether to laugh or cry from the absurdity of all the death around me. I now stay at home, between these four blue walls, and never go outside, with both my daughters, my husband, and my unborn child. I talk to them all the time, and they answer, as if they're still around; I hear their laughter and footsteps. My family has hidden all their photos from me, their personal things, but I don't need objects to remember them. They're with me everywhere, all the time. And at night after I've tucked my sons in, I go into my bedroom, alone with the memory of my husband and my daughters.

A few days ago, my little one insisted on going out; it started to pour while we were in the street. I don't know what happened to my boy, what scared him. He started shaking like a leaf. I tried to calm him down, like any mother would, to no avail. I stood where I was, the rain coming down, and me, in the street, remembering in that moment Aya and Raghad on the roof soaked in blood. Aya's eyes staring at me. Her terrified eyes staring at me and her younger sister's limbs draped over her; an image that will haunt me the rest of my life. I stood frozen in the

46

street, as helpless as I had been that day up on the roof, my son trembling. I don't know how much time I passed in that state. At some point a woman stopped and took my son into her arms, while I continued to stare at Aya and Raghad.

I try to hang on to life for the sake of my two sons, but there isn't much I can do. I just stay at home, inside, waiting for my family to come back, my family taken by war. But why is there war in the first place? Will they hear me if I yell? Will they bring back my daughters and my husband and my uncle and my unborn child? [*She wails; I try to calm her down. Her weeping is lost in the roar of shells landing nearby.*]

My life was so beautiful but they took it all from me. They've killed me. Destroyed me. [*She cries.*] But tell me, this war that killed my family, what is it for? Why all this death and destruction? What are they fighting over? What is worth all this death?

Neither of them have a reason actually, not Saleh and the Houthis, not Hadi. All of them are fighting for power, which in the end they'll just divide up, and all this blood will be forgotten. They aren't human enough to end this tragedy.

I lost the joy of my home, the lights of my life snuffed out. Now I'm in the dark. My daughters call out to me from somewhere, 'Mama, we'll be back. Don't be scared.' But now, I'm afraid of everything.

Munira Mahyoub Qaid al-Hamidi

At noon on Friday, 14 August 2015, the Houthi-Saleh militia targeted Abdulkareem Abdullah Abdelwahab's home in al-Tahrir al-Asfal in Taiz, with a Hauser missile. Munira's daughter Aya Abdulkareem Abdullah Abdulwahab (12 years old) was killed as well as her other daughter Raghad Abdulkareem Abdullah Abdulwahab (10 years old). Her husband Abdulkareem Abdullah Abdelwahab was shot dead on 12 November 2015, and her uncle Mohammed al-Haddad was killed at home on 21 March 2016 by shelling from the Houthi-Saleh militia.

WHAT HAPPENED WASN'T FATE AT ALL

I never see her in my dreams. Instead, the other women in my family dream of my cousin Leila, and tell me what she said and did. How they saw her rocking Nuhad, her daughter, singing her lullabies, songs we would sing in the evenings sitting in front of our tin shacks with palm frond roofs, cooling off from the heat, talking of days gone by, of a man's need to work and a mother's frustration after a long day, making them quarrelsome. In their dreams, Leila would be laughing at something or other in her head. The women would also talk of Leila's sadness in their dreams, exactly how she had been on her last day on this earth. 'I'm anxious,' she'd said that day. She'd known her time was near, we told ourselves afterwards. When the women of the family talk about Leila, I stay quiet; I'm as silent as I was that night my daughter cried out amidst the nightmare of fire that consumed our shacks. People I didn't recognize were trapped in the belly of the blaze. Cries for help; eyes staring into me.

When I ran outside the house, the sky was black without a single star, and only fires lit up the night; the flames reaching out their arms to nearby shacks. Cries for help, sobbing – I don't know what happened to me that day. I thought I'd been screaming for someone to save Leila and her family, but afterwards they said I'd just been standing at Leila's doorstep, frozen. That I hadn't spoken to them, that I'd just been staring into the fire. They'd been looking at me, concerned. When I yelled at the top of my voice, they said I hadn't yelled at all. That I'd been pointing to the scorched house, not a word passing my lips. But I remember yelling that night while I stood there, circling the flames.

Look, this is where Leila's house was. It shared a

boundary wall with the cemetery. Leila and her family burnt to death that night. [*She cries.*] I can still see the expression on Nuhad's face. Her soft baby skin blackened and her bones shattered before my eyes. When I saw her, I cried for Leila and remembered how happy she'd been when, after five gruelling years of trying, she finally got pregnant. We couldn't find Reynad, Leila's niece, that night; the blast of the rocket threw her tiny body far away. She was finally found outside the house, her burnt body torn to shreds. And when they pulled out Leila's body, I closed my eyes. I wanted to remember her as she always had been – a young woman bursting with life.

I never dream of Leila, but I see her when I'm awake; I see her on her journey of life, from our village al-Hussainiya[21] to the city of al-Hudaydah, a difficult journey, in search of safety. Leila suffered a lot in life: her husband couldn't find a house to live in in the early years of their marriage, so they stayed with Leila's mother for a year. There she fell pregnant and had her daughter, Nuhad. After some time, my brother insisted they live in his vacant house. That made us happy – finally, we'd be able to come together as a family in this place. It was land the state had given us when we came back from Saudi Arabia, after the first Gulf War. We built our houses here, side by side, with narrow passageways in between. We were happy, safe, making a go at life however we could, come what may.

That was exactly three days before they were killed. I still remember how happy Leila had been in those days: wrapped up in setting up her new house, singing while washing the floor, arranging furniture in the rooms – I'd hear her voice and smile. I didn't see her the day it

21 A village that falls under the administration of al-Jarahi district, in the governorate of al-Hudaydah.

happened, but the women in the family told me Leila had gone to visit her mother, her niece Reynad in tow. Just a few moments after they returned home, the missile hit the sewage pipe between our houses. [*Her eyes wander towards the cemetery.*]

Can you imagine? Firing a missile at our sewage pipe? Sometimes I laugh at it all; a missile, our sewage. Families in the neighbourhood said the Coalition had targeted the home of Darwish, the Houthi leader. We laughed until we cried. Darwish? Darwish, my father's brother, wasn't a leader, wasn't an official: he had never been interested in politics. He lived close by and was poor. His walls were destroyed during the attack and collapsed onto Leila's house. [*Nawal falls silent and looks around. Shacks are interspersed with gravestones. Worn-out mattresses peek out from several shacks. Children play in the sand, while three young men sit in the corner of the cemetery, absorbed in conversation. A clay wall, partly eaten away, stands between the cemetery and the shacks. From the room nearby, Nawal's father lets out a groan. I look intently at what had once been her niece's house, old burn marks visible on some of the stones.*]

Reynad's mother is still living with the shock of losing her daughter and sister. Sometimes she cries, and talks to herself, saying, 'It was fate.' Sometimes she cries out, 'It wasn't fate at all, the Coalition killed them! They were murdered in cold blood!' When we hear her wailing, we cry. Leila is buried in this cemetery here alongside Reynad; though Leila's husband and her daughter are buried in their village, far away.

Leila's murder and that of her family devastated our family. Since their murder, fear is all we know; we hold our breath in our homes, not setting a foot outside. One day I took my daughter, who is suffering from brain atrophy, to the al-Bahja Physiotherapy Centre. On that day,

51

before I got to the Centre, the Coalition planes bombed it. I don't know who was killed that day. This life scares me; nowhere is safe.

My young daughter Amina doesn't understand what's going on, but when she hears a plane up above, she has a panic attack, points to the sky and says, 'God save us.'

Nawal Abdullah Mohammed

At 11.00 p.m. on Sunday, 20 December 2015, the Arab Coalition planes fired a missile at the sewer in the al-Shuhada neighbourhood of al-Hudaydah. Nawal's cousin Leila Ahmad Saghir (27 years old), Leila's husband Ali Abdullah Wahish (30 years old), her daughter Nuhad Abdullah Wahish (three months old), niece Reynad Mohammed Ghayib (3 years old) and Nawal's neighbour Hameed Mohammed Ali (60 years old) were all killed. Hameed's wife, Saida Salim Ali (80 years old), was injured, and died two months later.

DEATH ON THE PIER

When I'm awake, when I'm asleep, I hear their cries for help. How many had there been? I don't know, but I do remember what some of them looked like: our neighbours from al-Tawanik mountain,[22] on the run like us. Hands reaching out to me. My son's head in my lap. I think of his head torn from his body – I see it growing bigger and bigger, taking up the entire sky. More dead bodies, and others taking their final breath. My other son bleeds out from an open artery. My daughter's crying pulls me back to my senses. I carry my injured son on my back and take my daughter by the hand. My steps are hesitant, faltering as my feet trample over corpses. I leave the bodies of my son and wife behind; I don't turn back. I hear crying and the roar of the waves crashing against the pier. [*He falls silent.*]

At dawn that day, our neighbours had told us that the mountain was about to fall into the hands of the militia, that they'd take the mountain by force, violating the sanctity of our homes. Missiles hit the opposite mountain, shaking the one beneath our feet. Panic filled the air like a restless spirit in the wind, and all the families started to think of leaving. We heard there were boats to take those fleeing to safety. I remember the darkness that swallowed the mountain; no electricity, no life now most of the families had left, only the sound of dogs barking into that beastly night, interrupted by militia shelling and air missiles. My family and I agreed to descend the mountain just as dawn broke, not taking anything but the clothes on our backs, leaving everything just as it was. Anxiously, we waited for the sun to rise.

22 A mountain located in the al-Tawahi district in the governorate of Aden.

At six we went down the stone steps, my daughter on my back, and my wife and two sons by my side. Our footsteps that morning still echo in my head. My daughter's heartbeat fused into my chest as we raced against time, and terror. You couldn't tell the difference between the sound of our steps and those of the dogs following behind. I was too afraid to speak; all I cared about was getting to the pier as soon as possible. I rushed my wife and children, trying to outrun our own shadows. I looked around me, and all I could make out that morning were our small shadowy figures and the mountain steps that we'd struggled down.

It was ten by the time we reached the pier, and other families had already gathered. There were hundreds of them. Like us, they were afraid, looking around with eyes full of worry. Like us, they had fled the mountains, whether our mountain, the one facing us, or from other nearby al-Tawahi areas. A few of them carried personal belongings, and others like us, had only themselves and their children.

I recognized our neighbour Waheed al-Mawz, his house had been above ours on the mountain. Their family had all come except for the grandfather who had refused, preferring to keep guard in the house. As I stood with my family, the first boat took off with twenty people. We felt hope at them being saved; our turn would come soon, we just had wait patiently. [*He falls silent.*]

The heat was unbearable; the sun rose and its rays started to fry our faces and scalps. Some men started chatting to kill the time. Women in a corner close to us began sharing their painful tales of war: the blockade, hunger, heat, blackouts – I listened to them, my eyes on the horizon. Something about the still air put me on edge. My daughter bounced around, pulling me back to what was around me. I kept my family in my sights, making sure my children wouldn't wander off. I don't know exactly when the wave flooded the pier and our bodies; I didn't hear the sound of the missile the militia fired at us, but I remember how we ducked and lay down on the pier shielding our heads and our bodies. A few minutes passed. Another missile in our direction. I covered my head and when I looked up, my son's head rolled into my lap. [*His voice catches and his eyes glaze over.*]

Have I forgotten something? I'll never forget, it all runs through my head like an unending war at sea between the ghosts of those who were afraid of dying and those who mercilessly kill them. Whenever I convince myself to give life another chance, preoccupied with my son's treatment and scraping together the money for hospital bills, my daughter who has only just turned three, reminds me of that morning. Sometimes she talks to herself, having a long conversation, and sometimes when we have visitors, she sits cross-legged and says, 'Baba, remember how Mama and Niyazi died? Houthis bombed Niyazi's head and killed Mama.' The more I try to make her forget, the more insistent she is on remembering. The victims' families will never forget those who were killed, and we, too, will never forget the faces of the killers.

Adel Ahmad Rassam

At 10.30 a.m. on Wednesday, 6 May 2015, the Houthi-Saleh militia targeted the boats of those fleeing al-Tawahi port in Aden. Dozens of civilians were killed, among them were Adel's wife Ibtisam Mohammed Abdu and his son Niyazi Adel Ahmad Rassam (10 years old). His other son was injured. All members of Wahid al-Mawz's family were killed, with the exception of the grandfather who stayed at home on the mountain.

THE FISHMONGER'S DITCH

I was hiding in a ditch, like a dog. I'd been there forever. My friend was already down there when the Apache helicopter gunfire started pursuing us through the desert. I remember rolling in the sand, trying to stay alive. The stones dig into my back and hands, my injured foot starts to bleed; in that moment I can only think of my brother Riyadh, but he was far away. I thought he was safe where he was, all I had to do now was make it through myself. When I'd reached the ditch, it had been pitch black, and all I saw on the desert horizon was Apache gunfire lighting up the sand and chasing nobody. [*He falls silent.*]

The stray dogs' barking gets louder; they smell blood. I see them gathered round bodies tossed onto the asphalt road. I'm curled into a ball and peek out at them over my knees. My friend comforts me and assures me that Riyadh must be fine. Riyadh has been bleeding out under the tree where we were hiding before I rolled here. I tell myself that he must be resting, probably collapsed into sleep, weak from pain. I observe the darkness around me, my life flashing before my eyes, gushing out any which way: as a child playing football in al-Jarr,[23] then as a father selling fish to provide for his six sons, father, mother, wife, and brother; I see them gathered laughing around me on holidays; my mother at the door praying for me like she always does before I leave for work; my little brother Riyadh swatting flies away from our fish, keeping an eye out for thieves.

Riyadh would often accompany me on my fish-selling rounds, especially on his days off from school, seeing it as a chance to explore new places. We start by buying fish

23 A village in the al-Jarrahi administrative district, governorate of al-Hudaydah.

from the Hudaydah Fishery – it's cheaper than the fisherman's market. After that, I store it in an ice box in my van, while Riyadh keeps an eye out for any kids who may take us by surprise and dash off with our fish. I drive with Riyadh next to me, his eyes lighting up at the sights on the road, or passively taking in the trees and passers-by, or resting gently, overcome by sleep. Riyadh never complains about coming with me to sell fish in al-Mazahin[24] or in the al-Jarrahi area; whenever he gets bored, he pulls out a schoolbook.

I look around me. I'm here curled up in a ball like a dog, next to my friend. The rattling of the Apache almost tears through my eardrums; ammunition belts dangle, circling over our heads, and a white light shines in our direction. Are they waiting for us to come out so they can kill us? I swallow my fears. My friend is silent, his eyes shining in the dark. Like me, he's probably wondering how we're going to make it out alive. The old man that lived in the usha[25] returns to my mind – he was the first to get struck by the Apache gunfire, and he rolled across the sand like us. His desperate cries still echo in my head, 'Help me! Somebody help me!' He must be dead now.

How long were we stuck in that ditch? I don't remember. What I do remember clearly is how we got there: I was driving with Riyadh in the seat next to me when we approached the coastline. It was morning, maybe nine o'clock, crisp, but sunny. We were singing and laughing, thinking about where to sell that day. When we turned onto the coastal strip, about half an hour away from al-Duraihimi coast, we fell into a trap; there was no going

24 A stretch of land in the administrative district of al-Adain, governorate of Ibb, central Yemen.
25 A hut made from wood or tin or palm fronds, used as housing by poor families in hot areas.

back. We were stuck. [*He clears his throat and groans in pain.*]

All along the coastal strip, cars and buses were on fire, trucks destroyed. A truck full of onions overturned on the highway, now smoking after being shot at. Afraid, we overtook it. We couldn't reverse because the Apache was shooting at any vehicle going in that direction. I started to panic. What was I going to do? We were stuck in hell. We couldn't go forward, back, or even stop. We kept going. A truck carrying a water tank had flipped over and burst into flames. Another huge one carrying I don't know what, partially blocking the way, was also on fire. I didn't see the driver; they were probably dead or had run away. I approached slowly and saw corpses scattered, I don't know how many: some of them charred, others ripped in two. Dead drivers and passers-by, dogs and cats along the coastal road, flies collecting round the rotting bodies. The air was heavy with an unbearable stench. We drove on. The Apache shot first at a truck a short distance away, and then turned on us. They got my tyre.

I carefully steered my car to park it by the nearest tree. Riyadh and I sat down under it. Eventually the Apache would have to stop shooting at us. I could then fix the car and we could carry on. But they kept on searching the area, firing at anything that moved. We stayed hidden under the tree. Time dragged on; our throats were dry and there was no food in sight. We were surrounded from eleven in the morning until nine at night when the Apache gunfire seemed to stop. I took a deep breath and tried to think of an escape plan, how to get out alive. But then the helicopter dropped a cluster bomb on the tree and took off.

The cluster bomb exploded into shrapnel, which grew smaller and smaller and smaller. I'd never seen anything like it. Death splintering in front of your eyes into ev-er-smaller pieces. The pieces pierced my body, and Riyadh was fatally injured. Do you know how a cluster bomb kills its victims? It explodes in the air into small deadly fragments, sometimes you can't even see them, and you think you're safe, but then you feel nails digging into your body, your flesh becoming a sieve. Blood was streaming from Riyadh's head; I propped him against the tree, and when I rolled into this ditch the Apache started shooting at the tree again.

I was so sleepy, my entire was body tingling. I had lost a lot of blood. I pinch my feet to stay awake, but my muscles are numb, as if a colony of ants is under my skin. I open my eyes and see shadows dancing out my life, my mem-ories, my death. Flies suck my blood, I swat at them, but they return, determined. I give in. I think of how set the Apache is on killing us – it wasn't enough for them to fire at us and chase us down, but they lay in wait this whole time, while we were hidden under the tree, then dropped the cluster bomb on us. What did we ever do to them? We're civilians, why do they want us dead? [*He cries.*]

I look at my watch, it's two in the morning. I've been down here five hours. The helicopter is gone. I don't hear it up above, nor do I hear the dogs barking. Have I gone deaf? But I hear steps stumbling in the sand, steps com-ing my way. My friend and two others I don't recognize, a torch shining in my face. 'Water, give me water,' is all I can get out. I drink. One of them bandages my foot. Hands of mercy carry me to the car. I hug Riyadh and cry bitterly. He's dead, motionless. His body cold, his eyes staring at nothing. They search for the usha old man, but there's no trace of him. My brother is dead beside me. The next thing I know, I'm in the hospital, with two women crying next to me, and I don't recognize them. I'm still in the dark. Rolling in that ditch until the end of time.

Mohammed Ahmad Daghmoush

On Thursday, 16 March 2017, Saudi Apache helicopters fired at the coastal line in the governorate of al-Hudaydah, killing dozens of civilians. At nine that night, one of the Apaches dropped a cluster bomb on those walking by the coast. Mohammed's brother Riyadh Mohammed Daghmoush (10 years old) was killed, and an older unidentified man. I visited Mohammed Ahmad Daghmoush in Amal hospital in al-Hudaydah. At the time of my visit, his wounds were still fresh and he was in severe shock.

A HOLE FULL OF NIGHTMARES

War has turned me into someone I don't recognize, some-one worn out by life, and now both mother and father to their children. Before the war, I didn't know what went on beyond our home; my husband was my only link to the outside world. But war tore me out of everything: myself, my family ties, my friendships. I'm now a different per-son, born from the womb of an unjust war.

The last week of April was the beginning of my devas-tation. It was the first year of the war when the first missile fell on the city of Taiz, hitting the workshop where my husband worked. I still remember every single detail of that day, like a photograph in my hands. In the corner of the photo is my husband Mohammed in his workshop smock, laughing.

My young son had been crying, as he'd wanted to go with his father. Mohammed kissed him and then quickly left with our older son without turning to see us again. But I remember his last look: his eyes rested on everything a little longer than usual, as if bidding the objects farewell. I closed the door behind them as I did every day, without any alarm bells going off inside me. No nightmares, no worries, no fears. Mohammed had convinced me we were better off staying here at home, despite the shelling that had started to target homes in our city. Even at its worst, the war would be more bearable here than in the village, and if we just stayed together, we would be secure enough to face anything.

The phone rings. Wrong number. It rings again. Silence from the other end, and then they hang up. I start to lose patience. Then more phone calls, relatives with conflicting news: 'Your husband and son have been injured,' 'They're both dead,' 'They're fine, just some minor injuries.' Then, a knock at the door. My uncle and sisters were on the doorstep, and I knew something unspeakable had happened. I begged them to take me to my husband and son. They had already been taken to Yemen International Hospital. We couldn't get to them; shells were falling on the city, and the transport to al-Hawban had been cut off after the militia took up position on the hill opposite the hospital.

My son Abdelrahman had been critically injured; shell fragments in his heart and spine had left him bedridden. Easing his physical pain was simpler than answering his questions about his father. When he asked, I pretended I was busy or hadn't heard him. I didn't tell him that I'd seen his father in the ICU after they'd cut off his leg because of gangrene, and that he'd died, leaving me alone. That day, they buried his amputated leg in the Kalabah cemetery in al-Hawban, and his body in the al-Ogainat cemetery. The thought of his leg buried in the east of the city with his body in the west always saddens me.

My mission in this life is for my son not to be disabled, but I can't afford his treatment, or to go abroad as the doctors recommended. I cry all the time; I don't know how to help him any more.

No one is helping us – not the Houthi opposition, not the organizations for the wounded, no one. They only look after their own; those from the same sect. As for people like us, they'll just let us rot and die from our wounds. When I see my son lying in bed, unable to move, or groaning on the cold nights, it breaks my heart. His silences send me into a fit of crying; what's going through his mind? I try to get him to open up, and sometimes he talks about his nightmares, how the missile just dropped out of thin air while they were safely inside the workshop, their bodies and their shoes flying through the air. His father had asked him for help, but he had been too injured to move, and was wracked with guilt. Sometimes he cries, protesting the war, and how unfair life is, but with time I've been able to sew up the hole from which such nightmares crawl out.

When you become everything for your family, the only way you can manage life is by depending on charitable people who know what a desperate situation you're in, or turning to your relatives. You have to do everything a mother and a father is expected to do, your back bending under the burden as each day passes. But when I think of all that I've been through, I can say that I'm strong. I go to the market on my own and buy things for the house: vegetables, bread, gas and medicine. Sometimes I have to fetch water from far-off places. Now, I take my children to school and come home with them. I train them to swallow this different way of life that I'm still wrapping my head around.

I know it's war that has made life so difficult for me and for many women in this country, but I don't get angry. I stay at home, locked up with my children, satisfied with these four walls protecting us from the outside.

Fatima Mohammed Salam

At 4.30 p.m. on Sunday, 26 April 2015, the Houthi-Saleh militia targeted the workshop where her husband worked, in the al-Sahaba neighbourhood of Taiz. Her husband, Mohammed Fare, was injured and died a week later. Her son has been disabled as a result of the attack. Fatima now lives in extremely difficult circumstances, trying every day to put food on the table for her children.

A BURNT SILVER RING

With eyes wide open, I stare at the blaze. It might as well be hell. I'm watching them run away: the managers, the gardener, both male and female workers, people whose faces I recognize, whom I speak to every day during my shifts at the factory, but in this moment it seems like they've lost their minds. They are running for their lives. I've forgotten their names; I've forgotten many things. What I do remember well is the stampede, their escape to the factory courtyard; then when the shrapnel fell, how they trampled over one another to the main gate leading to the road. Shielding his head, someone next to me mumbled, 'Oh God.' Ever since that miserable morning, the sound of their footsteps crunching the gravel has stayed with me. At first, I was like them, running without thinking, but midway, once there was distance between me and the fire, my chest tightened; I realized that my sister Faiza wasn't running like us, that she was still in the crisps factory. [*She cries.*]

Burnt images hover in my mind: a burnt life, the sad face of my father, my mother, and the wailing women mourning at our home float by, adrift. But what comes to me now is how everyone was running away from the factory that morning. I was running towards it, begging the first aid responders and the other workers to save my sister. I remember one of the workers yelling in my face, 'They're going to bomb the factory again! Can't you see the plane up there? Run!' No one paid attention to my cries. I went past the worker towards the factory floor. My sister Faiza was there with her workmates, Taqiyya and Salwa. She had always worked diligently, my disciplined sister. She didn't like to waste any time on her shift. Knowing her, she would keep working, no matter how dangerous it got. Hadn't she heard the missile crashing through the hangar roof? Hadn't she run from the flames like the others? Or was she just pressing her lips together like she always did when she didn't know what else to do? Finally someone told me that the missile had landed in the fryer with all that boiling hot oil – that's where Faiza worked – right in that hangar full of gas, diesel and cardboard boxes.

I ran to the hangar; I paid no attention to the yells of the workers, the plane up above, or the flames. A worker pulled my arm; I shook him off but he began to drag me back. I kicked him away along with everyone else who'd left my sister and her workmates to burn. They all thought I was hysterical, a friend said later, but I wasn't. In that moment, I was in my right mind and aware of everything going on around me. Making my way to the heart of the fire, all I could think of was my father's face. How would I answer when he asked me about Faiza? 'I left her to burn and escaped with the others.' How could I go home without her, when we had come to the factory together? When I saw the flames devouring the building, I wanted only one thing: to get inside and die there, next to my sister. [*She cries bitterly.*]

After I had been dragged out of the factory, I stood in the way of the bus about to depart. The general manager was on his way home bidding the workers farewell. I stopped him from going any further. 'Save my sister and the other workers!' I shrieked at him. I pulled him off the bus, but I don't know where he went after that. The managers are murderers, just like the Coalition's missiles that killed my sister and her workmates. They prevented the workers from getting out, leaving them to burn to death inside. The Aqel factory had been targeted more than once. That morning, before the Coalition's planes bombed it, the planes had hit the presidential house in al-Nahdein. We'd heard the roar of the planes followed by the bang of the explosion. At the time, we thought about going home because the managers had told us, 'When you hear the planes, just leave. Don't ask anyone for permission.' We gathered in the courtyard, afraid the planes would return. We went to Mohammed al-Khalidi, the factory supervisor, and asked him to get Yasser al-Aqel, the general manager, to give us permission to go home.

'There's nothing to worry about, but we'll get some buses to take you, just in case,' the general manager had said. We didn't see him after that. We then went to Saleh al-Mutawwa, the potato chips manager, and begged him to let us leave. He threatened us. 'If you leave now, don't come back tomorrow.' At the end of his sentence, the plane bombed the potato chips factory, and Faiza burnt inside with eleven of her workmates.

My other sister, Eman, was considering filing a case against the Coalition that murdered Faiza, and against the Aqel factory managers who caged the workers in like animals, saving themselves and leaving the workers to burn. But when my father heard this, he fell silent and looked off into the distance. I knew he was thinking of how difficult life has become without Faiza – she used to take care of everything. When Eman complains about the managers, he tells her, vulnerable and broken, 'My child, why would they listen to people like us?' I don't know, sometimes, like Eman, I think that all of those behind the deaths of Faiza and the other workers must be tried in court.

On that morning, we'd made rice with our female workmates. It was the first time we'd cooked in the factory – we always had an early lunch at our homes, which weren't far from the factory. I worked in the corn puffs

66

hangar, and Faiza was in the crisps hangar right across from it.

Earlier that day Faiza told us before going into the hangar, 'Wait for me and we'll have lunch together. Don't eat without me!' Those were the last words she said to me. After that I saw only her charred corpse. [*She cries.*]

We waited in the corridor of the German-Yemeni hospital. I stared at the corpses arriving one after the other: burnt bodies, unrecognizable, collected in black bin bags. Sometime later one of the hospital administrators informed us that Faiza and some of the other workers had been taken to the 'police hospital'. I knew that no one could have survived the factory fire, and that all the workers had burnt alive inside, but a part of me was holding out hope that Faiza had survived, just as she had when the factory had been bombed a few months before.

The police hospital hallway was packed with those injured from the factory bombing. I saw the supervisor who had stopped us from leaving the factory, and she was crying. 'It's my fault they're dead.' I didn't look at her – I was done with her and those like her. Black plastic bags were lined up one after the other; I couldn't keep count. I heard mothers and fathers wailing, and reassured myself that Faiza was okay. But that was when the morgue official asked me to identify my sister. [*She cries.*]

The basement was cold – there was no life at all in that godforsaken place, everything in the room was in preparation for death. I thought of the thousands of people who had passed through this place, whose families had had to identify them. I was staring at the corpse in question, looking intently at the pile of burnt disfigured flesh, and said to myself, 'It can't be her, it's not her body.' The lower half of the body before me was crushed and the upper half was completely burnt, as if it had been grilled. The insides of the lower part were spilling out. I looked carefully at the face: no eyes, no nose, nothing I could make out...it wasn't her. The hair was burnt. I touched it, and stopped. It was like Faiza's long, blonde hair; some strands were still blonde starting to look a bit copper. I looked at the fingers, burnt and shattered. And then I recognized the silver ring on her finger. [*She cries.*]

Every day, my mother sits in front of Faiza's bedroom door, crying while she remembers how Faiza had been angry with her the day she was killed. The night before, my mother fought with Faiza and until dawn and had gone to her room again and again, wanting to apologize. 'I had wanted to make up with her, but I kept stopping at the door,' she said to me. My mother has never forgiven herself for the fact that Faiza left this world upset with her. Feelings of guilt float alongside her words and paint everything around her in bitterness; her dreams are still haunted by the image of asking her daughter for forgiveness. Sometimes my mother walks in the garden, remembering her child and crying, sometimes repeating what Faiza used to say, 'As long as you have me, Umma, you won't need anyone else.' Then she goes into Faiza's bedroom, gasping with sobs enough to break your heart. Hearing her, my father seems older than his years. In those moments, in the darkness of my nightmares, a burnt silver ring shines.

Hafsa Hassan Mohammed Munawis

At 10.30 a.m. on Tuesday, 9 August 2016, the Arab Coalition targeted the Aqel potato chips factory in Sanaa. Twelve workers were killed, and among them was Hafsa Hassan Mohammed Munawis's sister Faiza Hassan Mohammed Munawis (20 years old), whose body was completely burnt.

The only way her family could identify her was from the charred silver ring on her finger.

THEY HAVEN'T LOST A SINGLE THING
IN THIS WAR

It is noon; in the middle of this war, I listen to my daughter singing to herself, the sound drowning out the rattle of gunfire and roar of shelling. In such moments, I think back to our neighbourhood where the ghosts of those killed by the fire[26] and shelling roam. The neighbourhood where I grew up, where through its windows flung open to the wind my dreams blossomed. The neighbourhood I left when I married, only to return with my daughter and husband during the war, only for us to live right above my parents' flat in the building in which I was born. Returning to the building where my family lived was a gift of fate; being near to my mother and siblings, I didn't pay much attention to the war.

It seems like a lifetime ago, how we would gather round the table, or huddle together on the dark evenings without electricity. We'd sit round and swap stories by candlelight, laughing like families brought together by war do, only to be torn apart later. I'd just become a mother, and was only beginning to grasp the mystery of this instinctive relationship with my child. I saw my mother and sisters in a brand new light; I took them into my heart, as if I myself had been born anew. But what does it matter now? Are you recording already? Wait a moment, give me a little time; I still need to warm up.

A few days and it would be Eid al-Adha. I remember the afternoon that day – we ate lunch at my parents' flat.

26 On 25 May 2015, when the city was suffering from an enormous fuel crisis, fourteen civilians were burned to death in the al-Dharba neighbourhood of Taiz when a gasoline truck exploded. Many people had gathered around the van to buy gasoline. Groups belonging to the anti-Houthi resistance were suspected of arson.

My brothers, sisters, parents, my daughter and me. After lunch, I went upstairs to my flat. My sister Marwa ran after me, kissed my daughter, and then left. My last memory is of how she looked that day, a halo of unforgettable light – she was vibrant. After she left, I busied myself with housework. I could still hear Marwa pestering my mother, 'You can all be my witness; she promised to take me to the souk!' I laughed at how mischievous she was; my mother could never say no to her. Shortly after Marwa and my mother left the house, I went outside to get some fresh air with Maha, my other sister who was in her final month of pregnancy. I hadn't been feeling stressed or anything, I had simply wanted to take a walk. But then Maha collapsed on the ground. I froze, not knowing what'd happened. I finally managed to calm her down and we started walking again. On our way, we stopped by a friend in al-Dharba al-Asfal neighbourhood. Still in shock, she told us about a missile that had struck in the middle of a funeral service at the home of one of her relatives. The dead man had fought for the Salafist resistance. She informed us that she had seen Abu al-Abbas[27] among those mourning. While she was speaking, shells started to rain down on the neighbourhood. We ran in the dark, racing through the rumble of the shells. I grew aware of a shadow behind me; it was my cousin. I was gripped by anxiety. 'Marwa's been injured,' was all he said. At that point I didn't know that my mother had been killed, and that my family were keeping it from me. [*She cries.*]

My mother and my sister were killed when the militia shelled Farah Mall in the al-Masbah al-Ala area. For my mother it was instantaneous, while Marwa was taken to the hospital, before passing away at dawn. This senseless

27   Abdo Fare, also known as Abu al-Abbas: a Salafist commander, leader of the Eastern Front in the city of Taiz.

71

war took both my mother and younger sister. My mother, the heartbeat of both our home and the neighbourhood. She was loved by all, and opened up her home to refugees and the sick. As if she knew her time was near, she absorbed herself completely in caring for those around her. I haven't visited them at the cemetery, because it was also bombed. Shells fell on the graves, throwing out the bones. Imagine, first, they killed them both, and then they chased them from the grave. What horror is this! [*She cries.*]

The worst thing is that they don't even give you the chance to grieve. I heard what our neighbours were saying about the clashes that day: the militia had shelled Bilqis school where fighters affiliated with al-Islah[28] had been gathered, and they had only done so in response to the resistance attacking our neighbourhood.

Yes, it's true that we used to hear gunfire now and again, but we didn't know what was happening. Others said the shelling by the militia was actually meant for the Abu al-Abbas convoy, but it doesn't justify killing civilians. But what does it matter now? My sister, mother and other innocents have been killed in this war. The war for them is nothing more than business – they steal the aid and keep it for themselves and their cronies. The victims' families in our neighbourhood haven't received any aid at all – can you believe it? Only those connected to al-Islah have. They haven't lost a single thing in this war; we're the ones who've lost everything.

Mayada Abdallah Ali al-Sabri

At 5.30 p.m. on Saturday, 19 September 2015, the Houthi-Saleh

28   Translator's note: the Islah Party or the Yemeni Congregation for Reform is a Yemeni Islamist party. It and the militias allied with it are fighting against the Houthis here. Al-Islah has received considerable financial backing from Saudi Arabia.

militia targeted Farah Mall in the al-Masbah al-Ala neigh-
bourhood in Taiz. Mayada Abdallah Ali al-Sabri's mother
Muna Sultan Saeed Thabit (50 years old) was killed, as well
as her sister Marwa Abdallah Ali al-Sabri (23 years old), and
three others.

HALF OF THE SUNKEN BOAT

Fishermen never set sail after sunset. Sunset means our day is done. We start our trips at dawn, or whenever the sun is shining. We move slowly, watching the tide and the movements of the wind; only when we're certain that the winds are suitable, with no storms on the horizon, do we sail out to deep waters. Our journey starts from the coast of al-Hudaydah and heads to the inner islands – the further out we go, the better the catch. After putting out the bait, we grab the fish that desperately thrash in our nets.

I can see us now: fish desperately thrashing for our lives. Us, injured, alone in the boat; others lost at sea. The night sea is frightening. Darkness upon darkness, a starless black sky, a sea that doesn't end with the horizon. Disorientated, I watch our boat drifting on its own. At times I feel the waves in my body as they gently push it ahead, at others, the barrels around us shudder, our bodies shaking alongside, and then sometimes the waves calm, all of a sudden, leaving the boat still. The sky spins hypnotically; I grow dizzy, fighting against losing consciousness and drowning. I shut my eyes and cling to the rope securing our bodies to the upper part of the boat, and anxiously watch the water as it pours into the already sunken half. I look at my two friends: they've been sleeping for some time, or more likely, they've lost consciousness.

We were eight fishermen from al-Jabaliyya.[29] At two in the afternoon we set out, the harsh sun beating down on our heads while we rowed far from the al-Hudaydah coast. The sea sparkled and our hearts buoyed in hopes

29 A village in the al-Tuhaita administrative district in the al-Hudaydah governorate.

of a large catch. We agreed to sail to al-Tarfah Island,[30] where the fish are plenty. Seeing the shoals below, we were happy, feeling that luck was on our side. We moved around deck excitedly, throwing our nets into the sea, chatting about our expectations for the day. Time flew. Out at sea, a fisherman loses track of time; his watch is set to how the waves move and how much fish he's caught. We hadn't noticed how late it was, but the sea was calm, and so we could go back whenever we wanted.

At eleven at night, we heard the roar of a helicopter above. But we couldn't see anything. A short while before, we'd heard guns fire into the sea. Later we learnt that an Apache had shot at a fishing boat carrying our friends. Their boat had been close to ours, but it was too dark to see anything. Terrified, we started rowing. Sweat poured from our foreheads and bodies. We rowed with all our might. We rowed against time. We rowed for our lives. But it wasn't long before the Apache helicopter started firing at us. The boat rocked back and forth and seawater flooded in; we all were wounded. At some point, I passed out from the pain, and when I opened my eyes, half of the boat was already underwater. I looked for my brother, my nephew and my fellow fishermen; I couldn't find them. [*He cries.*]

To this day, I don't know what happened to my brother Mohammed and our nephew Ahmad. Were they wounded? Or had they drowned like the others when the Apache attacked our boat? Had the waves swept their bodies away to a remote island, or were they buried at the bottom of the sea? All I remember is blacking out after they shot me. When I came to, my friends were securing

30   Al-Tarfah Island is part of the al-Hudaydah governorate, located near the al-Nukhayla coast in the al-Duraihimi administrative district.

my body to the barrels with a rope. My two friends and I were the only survivors, but we were all wounded, with no one to save us at sea. No coast guard, no one. The Apache attacked our boat and took off. We were alone in the boat. We were slowly sinking; our yells, sobbing and calls for help stifled by the vast sea. My hands, legs and head were injured but my grief for my brother, our nephew, my friends, made me numb to everything around me. More water poured into the sinking half of our boat. We waited for death. [*He groans in pain and then falls silent.*]

In between blackouts and sleep, I felt the boat drift endlessly through the night. I looked at the sky, and felt that time had stood still; we were the only ones left in this world, with only our moans of pain and the roar of the waves around us. When rays of sunshine began to brush my head, I half-opened my eyes. The sea was still, glowing with the blood of the dead. I opened my eyes wider to get a sense of where we were. Was the coast nearby? Looking around, there was only water surrounding us from all sides.

We were at sea for nine hours after the Saudi Apache shot at us. Five fishermen were lost, along with my brother and our nephew. We still know nothing of them today. Nine hours we were stuck in that sieve of a boat, drifting alone, wounded and having lost all sense of where we were. When awake, I thought of my drowned friends and family. My eyes were heavy; I opened and closed them only from time to time. At eight the next morning, the Djiboutian ship *Boto* found us by chance. They rescued us and we were brought to this hospital – as you can see, we are still here.

Ahmad Ali Abdalu

At 11.00 p.m. on Wednesday, 15 March 2017, an Apache attack helicopter from the Arab Coalition targeted a fishing boat by al-Tarfah island in the al-Hudaydah governorate. Ahmad's brother Mohammad Ali Abdalu (20 years old), his nephew Ahmad Mohammad Amari (18 years old), and his friends Abdelkarim Ali Jaber, Hasan Maafi Musa Jamal and Mohammad Hassan Yahya were all lost at sea. I met Ahmad in the al-Thawra hospital, in al-Hudaydah. He was wounded and in shock.

THIEVES AND RESCUERS

There's not enough light to make out what's around me. I'm pinned under the rubble, right up against the wall of the room where my daughters and nieces had been sitting. I can hardly breathe; dust and dirt fill my mouth and nose. I try to get up but the weight of the rubble prevents me. My husband is also under it all, and I see his niece, Ibtihal's head peeking out from under the debris. I hear her cry out, 'Aunty, help me! My foot is stuck.' I crawl in her direction, and try with all my strength to lift the weight of the fridge off her foot, so she can help me save her uncle. Just a bit more, just a bit more – I ask her if it's better now. She sobs. 'Aunty, my leg's going to fall off.' My voice is swallowed by the darkness. Laughter trickles in from the street, and I hear footsteps stumbling in my direction. Strange men whisper amongst themselves, rummaging around, looking for something. A light fastened to one of their foreheads illuminates the corners of the destroyed room. Thieves. One of them steps on Ibtihal. I yell, 'Watch it, the girl under you is still alive!' He turns to me, panicked. I beg him to save us. He and the other men start to dig around my husband's body, while I do what I can from my corner. The goodhearted thieves of war dig along with me. If it hadn't been for them, no one would have saved us, no one. Not the resistance, nor the Civil Defence, not our neighbours. If it hadn't been for these thieves of war, we would have all died beneath the rubble.

Just like that, after having fled to our family home in al-Hassib, afraid the militia would shell our area, our joy turned into sadness, our weddings into funerals. My nieces were happy to have the family together again, as Sana their cousin was getting married on Eid. Every day they'd go out to the souk and come back with more clothes to prepare the bride. But the bride, my daughters and all the other women in the family were murdered.

That day, their constant giggling had begun to get on my nerves. The house was packed with three families. I convinced my sister Anisa to spend the night at our other sister's house nearby. I remember my niece Sana hugging her mother lovingly and putting her shoes on for her. My daughter Maryam kissed me on my right cheek, and my other daughter Soumayya stroked my back. Maryam asked, 'Umma, what's wrong? You're chewing qat.' [*She cries, her voice catching. Her sister Anisa scolds her saying 'Crying won't bring our daughters back.*]

Those were the last words I heard from my daughters before they went into the other room. Then began the nightmare. At first it seemed like a beautiful scene: laughter, joyful trilling, everyone getting ready for their cousin's wedding, stacks of clothes, family gathering to celebrate...then suddenly life turned darker than it had ever been.

Corpses were piled up from the start of the hospital room to the end of it. I begged the nurses to let me see my girls, but they refused. I only saw them from a distance, unable to say goodbye like other mothers. I wanted to make sure that they weren't coming back. I didn't see them in their shrouds, take them to their final resting place, or kiss them goodbye. I didn't see them at their burials or in their graves. I only saw them from a distance through the crowds in the hospital. Were they really gone? I hung on to the hope that what'd happened had just been a nightmare, and that my daughters were still alive. I waited for them at our family home. I told myself, 'Maryam will come soon, Soumayya will come soon, I'll see them soon.' Maybe they'd been in the village and would come back to the house, their faces peering out from the hallway, laughing at how scared I was, and give me a kiss just like before. But when the days and months stretched on, and when they had been missing for a year, I knew that they were really dead and that I'd never see them again. [*She cries, and her voice breaks. Her sister comforts her until she calms down.*]

You don't know how draining life was for us. We were just trying to adjust, living every day in hope the war would end. But then disaster strikes and shatters you; the war broke me. But at what point do you realize that a disaster has taken hold of us all? I don't know, but now as I replay the events of those months – our fleeing and attempts to survive, then the murder of my girls – I know that the fates had planned their deaths.

At the start of the war, we were still living in our home in al-Hassib, my family on the first floor and Anisa's upstairs – our husbands are brothers. Our home was safe. But we were afraid the petrol station next to us would be hit. At that time, al-Hassib was under militia control, with snipers stationed on the high buildings, shooting whoever crossed the street. Families fled, fearing for their lives. And when the shelling worsened, we ran to the village, but the girls insisted on us returning to the city.

One day the resistance told us they would liberate al-Hassib in a matter of days. 'Don't worry about your houses, the resistance will secure the neighbourhood.' So we ran from our houses, leaving my gold and my husband's money behind. When we came back to the house, after my daughters' murder, the resistance had liberated the area, taking up posts. The locks to our home were broken. The resistance had ransacked everything: my husband's safe, my gold. It was the disaster that broke us, we had lost everything; our daughters, our nieces, and all we had worked for in this life.

When disaster strikes everyone at once, you don't know how to pick yourself up again. My sister's daughter was killed. Hayat, the wife of my husband's brother, was killed, along with their three daughters. Their sons' homes were destroyed. I lost my two girls and was left only with my son. His wife was injured from this disaster; her leg had to be amputated. She was pregnant at the time.

But do you believe in dreams? Signs we don't pay attention to, but that after a tragedy, we remember. Before Maryam was killed, she recounted a dream to me. She'd been walking through a narrow, deserted place, and couldn't breathe. Then it opened up, and the land became green 'like in heaven', she told me. [*She cries.*] I didn't remember her dream until after she died. But dreams don't tell us everything – they don't open our eyes up to what is coming. On the day it happened, I'd woken up in the morning in a panic. Something was squeezing my chest; I can't remember my dream exactly, but I do remember that something flew in from the direction of the shell, and I screamed until I could no longer breathe.

Our hearts are heavy and our spirits broken. Pain is engraved on our faces; just write what you see. I can't describe my disaster, just write what you see in our faces.

Tahani Mohammed Saif al-Qudsi

At 10.30 p.m. on Sunday, 23 August 2015, the Saleh-Houthi militia shelled the home of Abdo Dirham al-Qudsi (Tahani's brother-in-law) in the al-Merkezi neighbourhood of Taiz. Tahani's family had fled there together with the family of her sister, Anisa Mohamed Seif al-Qudsi. Her niece, Sana Mohamed Dirham al-Qudsi (27 years old), was preparing

81

for her wedding. The bride and both Tahani's daughters were killed: Maryam Mohamed Dirham al-Qudsi (18 years old) and Soumayya Mohamed Dirham al-Qudsi (15 years old). The wife of Abdo Dirham al-Qudsi, Hayat Qasim Numan (50 years old) was also killed, along with her three daughters Amira Abdo Dirham al-Qudsi (21 years old), Samira Abdo Dihram al-Qudsi (22 years old), and Amal Abdo Dirham al-Qudsi (15 years old). The call centre that the Abdo Dirham al-Qudsi family owned was destroyed when the militia shelled their home, and goods worth half a million Yemeni rials were burnt. The resistance ransacked the home of Mohamed Dirham al-Qudsi in al-Hassib. Anisa treated her daughter Ummat al-Rahman Jamil Dirham al-Qudsi, who had been wounded in the disaster, at her own expense. Still severely wounded, she had been discharged from the al-Safwa Hospital on the pretext that the contract between the hospital and the Saudi King Salman Centre had finished. I was able to speak with Samah Jamal Abdo Fare, Tahani's daughter-in-law, whose leg had been amputated. She was in the room with the girls when the militia shelled the house. She says that she only survived by chance; she had been lying under the rubble when a foot suddenly stepped on her. Her husband had tripped over her.

HIS EYE SAW WHAT HAPPENED

In the afternoon, I sit outside my front door, as I'm doing now, staring down the backstreets of our old neighbourhood, al-Hunud. I listen carefully to the footsteps in the alley, telling myself, *that's my brother Salem, that's Sabrine, that's Nujud, that's*...and that's when I realize the footsteps have already passed by. [*She cries.*]

Salem would come by every day – whenever he left his house, he'd come visit me. We live in the same neighbourhood, and we have lived next door to one another for a long time. The end of the winding alley through our neighbourhood opens out onto Salem's home; every day I'd wait for him to drop by. Sometimes when he'd come back from work during the day, we'd sit at the doorstep, taking in the roofs of the old buildings. Sometimes when he'd come back in the afternoon, we'd drink tea and tell each other our troubles. During the shelling, he'd come with his family. My nieces were scared and took comfort in being around my daughters, so he left them with me, saying, 'Girls, stay with your amma.'

That day, Salem came round as usual, his voice booming, calling out to me from the alley, 'Khayti,[31] what's on the menu today?' I'd made rice and fish. During the war, we got used to keeping our doors open to relatives. Together we'd fill our stomachs and console one another as much as we could. I still remember how his hands held the tea glass, quiet, much unlike himself, contemplating the neighbourhood as if engraving the images of the old buildings and their inhabitants on his mind. When he finally spoke, he said, 'I'm worried, Khayti.' I tried to lighten the mood, but he fell silent once again, and sat staring at the ground. Then he told his daughters, 'Come

31   Sister, in the Tihamiyya Arabic dialect.

on, let's go home, the shelling has stopped.' One of them, Aswan, pleaded to stay with me, 'We don't want to die.' None of us turned back to look at the other, like we normally did. I didn't stand at the door to see him off. [*She cries.*] When I turned my back on them, I heard a missile exploding. The walls of my house shook, and the ceiling caved in... [*Her eyes wander off into the distance.*]

I still remember that morning, how clouds of dust filled the collapsed house. I tried to get my bearings but couldn't see through. When I remembered Salem and my nieces, my heart stopped. I went out into the neighbourhood; houses were blown to pieces, some of them having fallen on those living inside. I looked around me and spotted Salem. He was on the ground, next to his wife and four girls, their bodies just a few footsteps from my front door. I stood where I was, unable to move. I yelled for someone to help them. I couldn't get to them – the hill of rubble from the houses was too great. A man from the neighbourhood carried away Aswan's corpse before my eyes, followed by the rest of the family. [*She cries.*] The neighbours came with lamps to save those trapped beneath the debris. I heard them counting the dead and the missing. My daughters dragged me out of the neighbourhood. I was like stone, staring at the spot my brother and nieces were murdered.

The Saudi planes killed my innocent brother and his family. Salem was just a simple employee at the al-Hudaydah airport, an errand boy concerned only with what was going on inside his home. He loved life; he dreamt of providing his family with a decent one, but the war killed them. His son Abu Bakr was the only survivor. He had been out of the neighbourhood that day. Whenever I see my nephew, I see Salem. Or when my thoughts run away with themselves in the morning or the afternoon, while

I'm cooking, I say to myself, 'Salem's nearly here, I see him on his way.' I see him while I drink my tea, I imagine him next to me. Then I remember he's dead, and I tire of this world.

I'll remember Salem till the end of my days: his face, his words, his dreams, our life as siblings together under one roof, then as parents anxious over our children. I'll never forget his eye that was injured by the shrapnel: open, alive, witnessing what happened to him and his family, damning the war.

Hajja Ruqayya Ahmad Yahya Qabih

At 9.30 a.m. on Thursday, 22 September 2016, the Arab Coalition's planes targeted a funeral in al-Hunud, a historical neighbourhood dating back to the beginning of the eighteenth century, in the al-Hudaydah governorate. The residents are poor. The missile killed twenty-four civilians, among them was Ruqayya's brother Salem Ahmad Yahya Ali Qabih (60 years old), his wife, Nujud Ayyash (50 years old), their daughters Asala Salem Ahmad Yahya Ali Qabih (16 years old), Hanan Salem Ahmad Yahya Ali Qabih (17 years old), and Aswan Salem Ahmad Yahya Ali Qabih (15 years old). Only his son Abu Bakr Salem Ahmad (16 years old) survived. Fifty other civilians in the neighbourhood were wounded, and thirty-two homes were destroyed.

A LOCKED ROOM FOR LOSS

I don't go to that corner of the house; the kitchen is next to that room. But when I have to go to the kitchen now and then, I don't stop by that room. It's been locked for a year now. I quickly walk past it without turning back. Sometimes I think I hear the girls laughing in there, or some movement inside – most of the time, though, I hear nothing. Our first day back at the house, three months after it happened, my husband unlocked the room. 'Let's leave it open so you get used to them not being there,' he said. But it was more than I could bear. I saw their bedroom door open for the first time since *that* day, and I was terrified. I tiptoed inside. Their things were exactly as they had been – time hadn't changed a thing: school uniforms still hung on the rack, a pencil on the table, certificates up on the wall, and pictures of them with me hanging in a corner of the room. Dust covered the frames; both of their beds were tidy as before. I slipped out, and locked the room never to open it again.

What I clearly remember about that day is holding both of them by their hands. The children were playing on the street as they always did at that time, and the sun on its way to setting. The way Rawan and Ula were laughing, it was infectious. I'd been waiting for them to come back from school so we could go for our weekly visit to my mother's. They were looking forward to visiting her at my brother's place and getting the chance to play with their cousins. Once they'd finished their homework, we headed out. My brother's house wasn't far at all. Time flew by and it was four-thirty by the time we left. On the way back home, Rawan and Ula were wrapped up in chatting about school, pulling me into their conversation now and then.

I didn't hear the shell explode. All I remember is turning behind me to finish what I was saying to them, then seeing them sprawled on the ground. I was in another world, it was like someone was shining a light straight in my eyes. I screamed and heard my own voice echoing in my ears. I was behind frosted glass, voices fighting for space, and then it was as if I was floating on air. But I wasn't – I was rooted to the spot, standing there looking at my two girls, not able to even take one step towards my brother's house to get help. I stared at them and wondered when they slipped from my hands. How did I get distracted? [*She falls silent.*] I don't know if they let go of my hands or if the explosion snatched them from me. There was less than a step between us. I always ask myself those questions and fail to piece it all together. I remember trying to finish what I was saying, then the next thing I knew they were on the ground. I didn't see how hurt they were, or how there had been a man behind me who'd been hit by the shrapnel and killed on the spot. I wasn't even aware of my own injury. I stood there, my eyes darting between Ula and Rawan's bodies, trying to move my feet, to take one, just one step towards them. But my feet had turned to stone. I tried with all my might to walk, and when I looked about me, it seemed that everything was frozen in time. My feet trembled and failed to carry me. Then I caught sight of my son. I remember his face as he made his way out from the smoke left behind by the shell.

I didn't think of all the strange coincidences that day; the change from our usual routine to visit my mother, us leaving the house late, how tense I had felt for some days. I thought it had something to do with the loneliness I felt after losing my father. He had been killed two months earlier by a sniper – we still don't know who did it. The phantom of death remained unseen, controlling our lives, without us daring to speak about it.

On our way to the hospital, night began to fall; I gazed at passers-by like a lifeless ghost. The blasts of the shells and rattle of gunfire brought me back to the war that had taken my daughters. I had no more tears, only pain lodged like a rock in my heart. In the hospital hallway, I saw my youngest daughter Ula, and when I started to approach her bed, the doctor took me out of the room telling me, 'We have to move her to al-Thawra Hospital, where her sister is. We've run out of oxygen here.' I remember my husband's sobbing lasting through the night, and I didn't know what had happened. None of them told me Ula was dead. They kept making excuses to keep me from seeing her. My back was bloody, but I didn't feel the pain of my wounds. I only learnt of my daughter's death on Friday, two days after her murder.

I didn't cry; I lost the ability to cry that day. I hung on to hope that my eldest daughter Rawan was still alive in the ICU unit. From behind the glass I'd stare at her endlessly, chasing away any negative thoughts, telling myself, 'She'll live, my girl will live.' They told me afterwards that she had opened her eyes just before passing on 10 January, four days after her sister. My grief is greater than my ability to face the emptiness left by their absence. I just keep staring into this absence, into the void that remains, mushrooming around me. I have no tears left to cry over how much I miss them; they dried up the day of their murder. I tried to get better for my only son and my husband. They were so relieved I had survived; I feel their anxiety for me. When my son wakes up at night, I hear him make his way towards my bed – he stops there and makes sure I'm asleep. In those moments I push down my grief.

I don't know how other mothers cry. I have no tears left;

I have nothing except defeat. I look at the locked room all the time, and think of how I'll keep it closed to preserve their precious souls forever: their small dreams hanging on the walls, pictures of them scattered here and there. The room is locked, I think of them and challenge myself to pass by. I hear their voices coming from somewhere far away and it gives me the comfort to carry on.

Intizar Radman al-Qabati

At 4.30 p.m. on Wednesday, 6 January 2016, the Houthi-Saleh militia dropped a shell near the Jordanian University in Taiz, where a group of children were playing. Two children were killed instantly: Ula Arif Ali Murshid (10 years old) and Mohammed Waheeb Abdallah (16 years old). Intizar's other daughter Rawan Arif Ali Murshid (14 years old) was fatally wounded, and died on 10 January 2016, four days after her sister. Intizar was also wounded by the shrapnel. At first, she refused to be recorded or give her testimony; she was in severe shock.

DO I COVER MY EARS OR THEIRS?

Sometimes I lose my grip on reality. In those moments, I don't know where I am, or what I'm doing there. When I make my way back to myself, I remember the children I still have. I panic. What happened is more than I can bear; it's only my children who keep me from losing my mind completely. [*He looks at what is left of his home.*] Look.

Here's where the door to our flat used to be; the missile tore in through here, and this hole is from another strike. Our building was hit again on the second day of Eid. [*His mind wanders. I try to get him to speak. His voice catches and he cries.*] When I sit on the debris from my house like we're doing right now I'm stricken with madness. I lose my mind when I search for the remains of my family's bodies. I see their eyes staring into me, I hear their screams in my head. When I finally escape these dark thoughts, I find myself drenched in sweat. I rented a flat near here so that I could be close to my family.

Most of the time I sit here, contemplating the pile of rocks, seeing my life now as the rubble of a prior existence: brick, cement, rock, and nothing else. I close my eyes, and when I open them again, I see people passing by just as they've always done – going to work, carrying on with their lives without a second glance at the debris that remains of mine.

A few days earlier, I made my own blood run cold. I was driving my bus in al-Hawban, when I met one of my friends by chance on the road. I don't remember his name now. He told me, 'Hashim, let's go to Bir Basha.' I got into the minibus with him and forgot all about my own bus. I didn't realize until a friend called to let me know that it still was in al-Hawban. So I went back – or at least I tried to, because suddenly I found myself on a bus going somewhere else entirely, to Waza'iya. [*He laughs.*] Do you think now that I'm in my right mind? Hardly. Shock drives a person to madness, when he thinks of how he's lost everything he was living for. I don't know what to do. How can I stay sane and stable? How can I push myself to keep going?

It was on the day of Arafat, just one day before Eid al-Adha. I don't remember the exact date – my memory can't hold much of anything any more. The city streets were buzzing with life, people out in front of shops buying sweets, getting ready for Eid. Just ordinary things; families resisting the war and the blockade. My family had just returned that day, having left a few months before for the village. But they were going to travel back once more to spend Eid far away from the war, the sound of shelling and the air raids. But my family's dreams for their lives and of spending Eid in the village vanished that afternoon. My wife went up to our flat with my eldest daughter Khadija and my son Ziyad, leaving the rest of our children at my brother's house. 'I'll just get the children's clothes,' she said. I followed them, planning to shower and change my clothes before fetching lunch from outside for us to eat together. But my wife and daughter said they were fasting. With a tightness in my chest, I stepped out with my youngest son to have lunch somewhere, and then come back home.

I was in my workshop near the house. At eleven in the morning, I heard a deafening roar. I ran, not looking ahead or behind. I remember now the terror I felt when I reached the road which housed the building where we used to live: people were gathered there, talking loudly and shouting, but I couldn't understand a thing. And why were they standing in front of my home? My feet weren't strong enough to carry me. I elbowed my way through, getting closer to the building. Some of them tried to stop me, but I fought them off and kept running. [*He cries.*] But there was no more building, no more flats, no one inside, just rubble. Piles and piles of rocks. I remember the moment my eyes landed on all this – I wish I had no memory at all. When in a matter of seconds you find that life as you knew it is now in ruins... [*He cries, beats his chest. I try to calm him down.*] Before me was what remained of the flat: the roof of the building, the outer walls still in place, a wall of a room hung loosely in the air, the stairs leading to the flat, in pieces. Everything gone in an instant; a crater in the depths of the earth is all that remains of my life. I looked around me in disbelief and searched for my wife and children – I couldn't see them. I never thought for a moment that they were dead. [*He cries.*]

After some time, the neighbourhood families began pulling corpses out before my eyes in severed and crushed body parts. My daughter Khadija's foot, and then my son Ziyad's hand, and my wife's remains mixed with the soil. I stared and stared at what was around me, and panicked, refusing to believe that I had lost the love of my life. Eighteen years passed before my eyes. Memories flooded before me: our love, our life together, our dreams, our conversations, our joys, our sorrows. I remember it all and cry bitterly. I remember my first seed, my first bud of joy: my daughter Khadija. I remember how she was when she came into this world, a small bundle looking curiously around her. Ziyad, my eldest son, the crutch I used to lean on. Suddenly they were gone, never to return. What does anyone gain from this? [*He cries.*]

Sometimes I imagine that none of this really happened, that my wife and children are alive somewhere else in the world. But when I pass by our home each day – and spend hours lost in thought, staring at the rubble – I remember my wife's laughter, my children playing, our mornings together: them going to school, me to work, my wife busy with chores. I remember that life and can't find it any more. [*He cries.*]

The Coalition's planes killed my wife, my daughter Khadija and my son Ziyad. I can't understand why. What did they do to deserve it? They weren't armed or sided with any part of the war; they were civilians. I was just working to feed my family. I'm not into politics and I don't support either side in the war. Look at this building – we used to live here. Civilians minding our own business. There weren't any armed men here or any military check-points, just an ordinary building with ordinary people in it. They thought they were safe, getting ready for Eid, and the Coalition murdered them. Rescue workers searched the rubble for valuables, stealing my wife's gold and my bus papers. Imagine! Suddenly you lose your family, your life, everything you spent more than nineteen years working for, as if all you'd been doing was digging this crater here.

A few days after it happened, I dreamt of my wife. She was wearing a white robe. I cried and told her, 'Don't leave me alone, I can't live without you.' [*He cries.*] She responded, 'Stay for the children.' I wake up, my heart heavy. I pull myself together for those still here. But when my young daughter calls me and tells me sobbing that she wants her sister Khadija, I just don't know what to tell her. [*He cries.*] When I hear my children crying any time a plane passes over us – reminding them how their mother and siblings were killed – it's like my heart is being squeezed. I don't know how to make them any less afraid – do I cover their ears or mine?

I no longer have a life; no home, no job. My children are homeless, living in the village now with their grandmother, forever missing their mother and siblings. I try to be strong for them, but in the blink of an eye you realize you've lost everything: your wife, your children... I've lost my wife, the love of my life, who gave me strength. If only I could bring her down from heaven right now. But it's not up to me. [*He cries.*] These people don't leave anyone to grieve in peace. Imagine, they made excuses for the Coalition bombing my home and killing my family. I heard such things and swallowed my anger. A few days after it all, I was on my way to my destroyed home and heard a passer-by point at the remains of my home and say to his colleague, 'The woman who was killed in the building was the wife of a Houthi leader.' My wife! When I heard this, I couldn't control myself any longer. I took out all my anger and resentment on him. [*He smiles.*]

How can they deny that we're victims? I'm only one of the thousands who have lost their family in a Saudi airstrike, but each time they go on justifying the killings, downplaying our tragedies. However much they deny it all, God in heaven knows what they've done to us. Now you see my disaster before you. There are so many like me, but no one knows their stories, no one wants to hear them. The day after the killing, the leader of the al-Islah Party, Dia al-Haq al-Sami, called me and said, 'They're still repeating their mistakes.' I didn't say anything to him. Instead I sent him pictures of my dead children. 'What did they ever do to deserve this?' he said. Too little, too late. They don't let you heal from your wounds; they do everything to cover up their crimes. Imagine, for the crime committed against my family, no one came to check on us, no committee met, no official or politician enquired about what happened to us. Nobody cares about the victims. They don't see victims as human like them, people who had a life of their own before they were killed for no reason. Even the aid, they kept it for themselves. They don't for a moment think about children in need. The Islah party stole the aid, and distributed it among their friends and family. Write this down – I'm not afraid of anyone and I don't want anything from them. I lost my family, my house, everything I worked for. Even the workshop where I used to work, next to the airbase, was bombed by the Houthis. And now I have no work, the workshop has been lying idle for two years. But there are families in need. A very dear friend of mine lost his family in a Coalition air raid. On the phone he asked, 'Did you actually get any relief supplies?' I felt so sorry for him.

What should I do? Where should I go? My life is now in ruins. Then again, when I see the misfortune others are going through, I stay quiet, and remember a labourer that I had. His entire family was killed in an Allied air strike. Mother, father, siblings and his brother's children. Eleven people in all. I remember that day – I held him tight to stop him doing anything to harm himself. I thank God that I still have four children, that they didn't kill them all. Sometimes I laugh bitterly when I see my life now. I make an effort so that I don't lose my mind, but who will bring back my family, my wife and my children? Sometimes I speak to myself, a long monologue that I only wake up from when my remaining children and friends pull me back to reality. They're the ones keeping me sane.

Hashim Mohammed Thabet Hajib al-Qudsi

At 11.00 a.m. on Wednesday, 23 September 2015, the Arab Coalition's planes targeted Hashim Mohammed Thabet al-Qudsi's home in the al-Dehi neighbourhood of Taiz. His wife, daughter Khadija Hashim Mohammed (13 years old) and son Ziyad Hashim Mohammed Thabet al-Qudsi (9 years old) were killed. Rescue workers stole all he owned that day. We sat on the remains of his home and I recorded his testimony. He cried throughout the entire recording, and kept asking me, 'What should I do to stay sane?'

'I just want them to shoot me in the head.'

'Why, my boy? Then you'll be dead and they'll cover you with dirt.'

'Well, I want to die. I'm done.'

'Who upset you? You have your toys, your new clothes. And you're still going to school. One day you'll be a doctor.'

'No teacher, no doctor, I don't want that. I don't want anything.'

'But if you die, you won't see your friends any more!'

'I know. When people die, you put them in the ground and the worms eat them.'

'Why are you saying things like this? What's wrong? Why are you thinking like that, darling?'

'I told you, I'm done.'

I remember Anas's words now and cry. Like knives, they twist deep into my heart. That day, I didn't understand why all he could think about was death. Had the illustrations in his schoolbooks frightened him? I went to his school to find out. The way the teachers screamed at the children scared me, but it wasn't the pictures in his books that awoke the idea of death in Anas's soul. Maybe it was when he was at his uncle's house in al-Hawban and his aunt was killed by a sniper? Anas stayed there six months right in the middle of the air raids and the bombardment. Maybe the war terrified him and he just wanted to die instead? No, it was none of that.

Anas was older than his years; he thought of things other children didn't. Looking back on his last days, he was silent. He wanted to be alone and was restless. He'd left his toys with his friend, our neighbour's daughter, and had many projects that preoccupied him, which he would abandon the next day: buying a camera, then a large bicycle, then suddenly deciding to sell it and save the money for another idea flying round his head. Sometimes he would collect the broken locks from houses in the neighbourhood that the owners had discarded, saying 'I'll sell them after the war.' Other times he'd collect shell casings and the remains of other projectiles, thinking of how best to use them. But in his final days, he was silent and fed up with everything. Was this a sign or just a coincidence?

Since Anas's murder I've been going back over these details again and again; all of it is cloudy now. All that remains is the taste of immense grief. The night before it happened, Anas had gone to bed unusually early. We'd usually sit together and have fun. He said, 'I want to sleep now.' I asked my husband, 'What's with Anas these days?' I didn't sleep that night, exhausted from pain in my womb. In the morning, everyone in the house got up, but I stayed in bed. I heard noise coming from the kitchen – my daughter was making breakfast for everyone. I couldn't bring myself to get up, as if some strange force was pinning me to my bed. I waited for my favourite morning ritual: Anas would come into my room and give me a boost. But Anas didn't come into my room that morning – he remained standing outside. He didn't smile and pretended to be busy. Then he asked if we needed water; he could fetch some from the tanker in our neighbourhood. 'We have rainwater,' I told him. He grew angry and mumbled some words I didn't catch, then slammed the front door behind him.

Sirens, screams, running. The rumble of another shell closer than the one before. Our house shook and the corridor filled with smoke. A black cloud blanketed everything: voices, the furniture, life itself. That's when I remembered Anas out in the street. I had always forbidden him from going outside during the shelling. My husband Abdeljaleel came inside with Anas in his arms. My eyes focused, not comprehending what was going on. I looked at my husband – his clothes were soaked in blood. Anas was laid out on the floor, and my husband was trying to stop the blood. I ran like a mad woman, bringing towels, handkerchiefs, anything I could get my hands on to stop the flow, but it kept gushing out. I yelled at my husband, 'He's dead!' He assured me, 'He's not dead, he's probably unconscious.' I don't know what came over me, but I started crying out, 'It's your fault, you killed Anas. Why didn't you bring him inside earlier? Why did you leave him outside?' Then I came back to my senses and tried with my husband to stop the bleeding once more. Anas raised his head and looked at me the way he did – that look still haunts me. His head then flopped down on his neck, and I knew that he was dead. [*She cries. Her voice catches. Her husband tries to calm her down. He tells me, 'Stop the recording.'*]

What do they want from us? [*She cries.*] The militia have killed our children, our sons and our daughters, our men, our women. We live every day in fear. At night we lie awake dreaming of our children. You and those like you make us relive our sorrows and then don't do anything for us. Whenever one of you visits me, I go back into my depression. Tell me, what can you all do for us? Nothing. We don't want money – that won't bring my son back. What I want is for his killers to be brought to justice. Can you make that happen? I didn't think so. I'll never forget my son, but you keep reopening our wounds only to disappear. [*She cries.*]

You can't imagine the pain of losing your youngest

child. You don't just lose your connection to life; your life loses all joy and meaning. My other children were jealous of my love for Anas, complained that I spoiled him, giving him whatever he wanted. I told them, 'You're older now, and each of you have your own lives. We've already raised you and gave you whatever you wanted. Now, you don't need us any more, but Anas does. He's what still gives our life meaning.'

The militia killed my son. The neighbour's daughter cried over him and refused to go to school. But it wasn't long before she forgot her friend. Children forget quickly, but we adults never do. When I hear children playing in the neighbourhood, I remember Anas and I tell myself, 'Anas would be doing such and such. He'd suggest an adventure to his friends. He'd run to the end of the neighbourhood, with the other children trailing behind him. He'd laugh while cheekily teasing them. There's no one like my darling Anas. Then he'd come into the house and say, 'Mama, give me some juice. Mama, the death game is sad. Mama, I don't want to die.' [*She cries.*]

Naima Ali Ghalib

On Tuesday, 1 December 2015, the Houthi-Saleh militia bombed a water tanker in the al-Kuwait neighbourhood of Taiz. Three children were killed: Naima's son Anas Abdeljaleel Mahyub (7 years old), Asma Abdo Ghanem (15 years old), and Shayma Adel Mohammed Sayf (13 years old).

I SAW HER... SHE WAS DROWNING

I looked for her everywhere on the boat, but I didn't find her. Had the sea split open and swallowed her whole? My friend, Salma Kis, often appears to me in my dreams. I see her exactly as she was on our journey from our country to Yemen. The saddest thing for me is that I don't know what happened to her. I asked our friends who did survive about Salma, but no one had seen her. I keep thinking of the plans we had chattered so much about as neighbours back home in Somalia. All we dreamed of was the life that awaited us, a life unlike the one of war in our country. Three months ago, we made a plan: after coming to an agreement with the smugglers, we pooled together all our savings, borrowed some more, and sold all that we owned – all so that we could leave Somalia. They said they would get us to the Yemeni coast, but that we'd have to wait there until they organized our journey by sea to Egypt, and from there to Libya. After that we'd start the final leg of our journey to our dream destination.

I don't remember exactly when we reached the Yemeni coast, but I do remember how happy we were: taking the first steps towards the place we'd been dreaming of. I remember how the cool sand felt beneath my feet, seeing the clear blue sky up above, and hearing the cawing of the crows by the shore. In that moment, I felt life was finally smiling at us. We were ready to face whatever came our way – which is why we weren't disappointed when they moved us to Kharaz camp.[32] It was a place for us to catch our breath before continuing onwards. In the camp we counted the days and minutes till our next journey. In our tired eyes, all the days and nights blurred together. Then

32 Kharaz refugee camp located in Ra's al-Ara, in al-Mudharaba administrative district, Lahij governorate.

everything changed: we got news our boat was about to leave.

The boat set sail at two in the morning. There was no sound for miles around, only the sand crunching under our feet and the roar of the waves. The boat was jam-packed with one hundred and forty Somalis. Women, men, children, the elderly – all squeezed onto both decks of the boat. Fatigue took hold of our bodies and spirits. Each of us was thinking of what we had gone through to get on this boat and of the future that awaited us. I was exhausted, but I let myself be carried away by my dreams that I saw sinking in the darkness of the sea one minute, then floating on the foam of the waves the next. Darkness enveloped everything, except for distant stars in the sky. Silence was interrupted only by the crashing of the waves. The most exhausted fell asleep first. Some of them lay down on the deck, while others curled up next to their belongings. The snores of the elderly drowned out the moans of the mothers, their hungry children, and the voices of young men chatting about their future plans in the corners of the boat. I fell asleep unaware of anything around me. Now and then, I was jolted awake by the boat or a fight that had broken out somewhere on board.

At noon, we heard the occasional buzz of an Apache helicopter, but couldn't see it. None of us paid much attention to it. The children were getting up to no good on the deck and the women laughed at their mischief. Time flew by. After a good fifteen hours at sea, the helicopter flew closer to the boat. Then it came down very low, and at around seven in the evening the Apache helicopter opened fire on us. Our dream quickly became a nightmare.

I remember our terror when the helicopter started to chase us on the open sea. It fired indiscriminately at the roof of the boat. The children's cries and the elderly's screams grew louder. We tried to escape the Apache's bullets, but how could we flee death as it chased us across the open sea.

At first, I stood next to the captain. For some reason I thought the Apache wouldn't shoot at him. But when the bullets combed the back of the boat and started to get close to me, I ran. But there was nowhere to hide. Everyone was running panicked. We stepped on each other's feet, stumbling and falling over one another. Everyone on the upper deck was killed. For those who were hiding on the lower deck, the only safe place they found was the belly of the ocean. I searched for my friend Salma, but I didn't see her in the chaos. I saw men who jumped into the sea of their own free will and others who rolled in unintentionally. A twenty-something-year-old man tried to flee the gunfire, but his head was split open. I saw the owner of the boat when the bullets severed him in two. Bodies were lying everywhere. You couldn't move your feet without stepping on someone.

The captain turned off the engine in the hope that the Apache would stop firing. The boat lay on the water for three hours. I listened keenly, looking for somewhere to hide. I curled up under the corpses – two of them had been friends of mine, refugees like me. The other bodies I didn't know. The dead bodies were my shield, absorbing the Apache gunfire. In that moment I thought of death and surrendered to my fate. When the rattle of the helicopter stopped, I lifted my head and sighed. But the Apache came back again, raining gunfire on our heads. Again, I hid under the bodies. I remember the sheer terror of the men who carried children on their shoulders, their trembling small hands waving to the helicopter. Crying, raising their voices, 'We're Somali. We're refugees. Don't kill us; no guns here!' But the gunfire didn't stop, three hours straight they had been shooting at us. Finally, it pulled away. The captain started to slowly steer the boat through the dark night and the wide-open sea. Faceless corpses were all we could see. The smell of blood filled our noses. The groans of the wounded and their cries got louder through the night. I was wounded too, but I didn't feel the pain. With my eyes half closed, I watched the captain. And whenever he switched off the engine, everyone held their breath.

A fearful eternity passed before we reached the shore. Again, I searched for Salma among the bodies and the wounded. I didn't find her. To this day, I don't know what happened to her, but I know only too well what happened to our dreams. They drowned in the sea.

Muna Awad Mahmoud

At 7.00 p.m. on Thursday, 16 March 2017, a Saudi Arabian Apache helicopter shot a boat carrying Somalian refugees. Forty-one of them were killed, ten others were lost at sea. One of them was Muna's friend Salma Kis (18 years old). Muna herself (20 years old) was wounded along with dozens of refugees, some of them fatally. The wounded reached al-Hudaydah fishing port where they were transported to hospitals by fishermen. The militia detained seventy refugees in the central prison and moved the women to a camp in the city.

THE ACHE THAT DOESN'T GO AWAY

My son Majd was killed the moment the shell hit the square. His body burned. Later, I was told he melted. I clung to the hope of my other son Muhannad being saved. The whole night he was delirious: people without heads or with burnt-off faces chased him with knives. They were trying to kill him. Others were hidden in the fridge of his hospital room, waiting for him to fall sleep so they could take revenge. He sees them, not us. He speaks to them, curses at them. We try to assure him that no one is after him and that we're right beside him, that he's safe. The doctors told us he was hallucinating and that we'd have to be patient.

Four days after Majd's murder, I left the mourning women at home and told myself, 'One is dead, we've got to save the other.' I was giving myself a glimmer of hope, however small, to keep fighting. It wasn't an escape from my grief, but rather an attempt to save my other son. I remember those days now, how I stayed in the hospital next to Muhannad for months on end. I was an obsessed nurse, desperate for my son to live. Muhannad had third degree burns, and he'd follow his brother Majd in death the moment I took my eyes off of him. A woman obsessed, I ran after the indifferent doctors, begging them to save Muhannad. I knew how weary they were from the everyday murder in this city; they didn't pay attention any more to victims' families crying for help. But I didn't give up. I was a wounded mother ready to take on the world to save her youngest.

After months, the doctors convinced me that Muhannad had to be transferred to Sanaa, otherwise he might lose his foot. Shrapnel had torn apart his skin, joints, tissues, and tendons. He was too young to be disabled. I'd stare at his small burnt body: face, lips, eyebrows, hair, back, and a foot that might have to be amputated. When I looked into his eyes, I saw the fire, I heard victims screaming. I saw Majd's face and Muhannad's horror at seeing his beloved brother killed in front him. Jolting awake from time to time, he'd ask me about Majd. I'd answer, 'Your brother is in the ICU.' He insisted on seeing him. I gave the excuse that, 'Your brother is in critical condition, they're taking him to Sanaa for treatment.' I was afraid to make him face his brother's death. I myself hadn't yet comprehended the loss. How would I be able to console Muhannad? I'd have to go through it all again. When we got to the hospital in Sanaa, the first thing Muhannad said was, 'Mama, we're in Sanaa now, I want to see Majd.'

'My boy, they've taken him abroad.'

His face lit up, 'That means he has a chance of getting better.'

I knew in that moment that all I was doing was tightening a noose of delusions round his neck. I finally broke down crying, 'Your brother is dead, Muhannad.' [*She cries. Her wailing grows louder. Her daughters also cry. Her husband consoles her, and she quietens.*]

I will never forget his comforting words, 'Mama, don't cry. You've lost one son, but God has saved your other one. But what about me? I've lost my big brother who was everything to me.' We cried together, a grief-stricken mother, her son who escaped death, her husband and three daughters. We wept together bitterly, as if Majd had just died in that moment, and from his beloved body Muhannad had come forth.

Children don't understand how irreplaceable each child is to their mother. Even if you had a dozen of them, it's as if you've lost a part of your soul that can never be replaced. You remember your child in your womb, you remember the days and nights you lay awake thinking of what he would look like and what his future would be. Children don't know this pain. My joy at Muhannad's survival doesn't ease my pain of losing Majd.

I think of him all the time. Majd wasn't like other children his age. He was my eldest, my firstborn, seventeen years old. He was full of life, raring to go, a child who had skipped childhood and gone straight to his teenage years, with the naughtiness of boys and sibling rivalry. He would bicker with them and always be one-upping his siblings. I would get angry at such behaviour. Now I know that I tired him out with all my grumbling, and that I didn't trust him enough.

I was terrified when Majd told me he wanted to get a gun and join the resistance. I felt like I couldn't breathe. I imagined Majd stretched out on the ground, soaked in blood, like thousands of other youth who had been killed in this war, whichever side they were on. All that is left of them is a photograph passed round for a while, then they're forgotten while the grief crushes the hearts of their mothers. I didn't know how to get the idea out of his head. I told him there were other ways of supporting the resistance, but he wasn't convinced. I told him, 'When you're twenty, you can do what you want. But right now you're still my child.' The image of Majd on the ground in a pool of blood stayed with me. I forbade him from going out. And when he did, I monitored his movements so that he wouldn't go too far. But I realized after his murder that you can't cheat death – all of my maternal precautions didn't stop the war from taking Majd from me. He was killed just in our neighbourhood. [*She cries.*]

A few months after his death, I saw Majd in a dream. He was beautiful. I cried like a tormented mother who has lost her son, but then finally finds him. 'Son, they told me that you were dead.' He smiled at me. 'Forgive me, Umma.' I ran to embrace him, but a sharp pain in my stomach snapped me out of my dream. My chest tightens whenever I remember Majd, although I believe we should accept our fate. Even though my husband and I have been so preoccupied with saving his brother – we had to sell all that we own – and yet, Majd remains the ache that just won't go away.

Samira Mohammed Abdalwase

At 4.30 p.m. on Thursday, 20 August 2015, the Houthi-Saleh militia shelled a group of children in the neighbourhood of al-Qarya, in the Asifera district in the governorate of Taiz. Samira's son Majd Mutahhar Hizam Mohamed (17 years old) was killed and her son Muhannad Mutahhar Hizam Mohamed (13 years old) was severely injured, as were other children. The family was forced to sell all they owned and borrow money to save Muhannad. The government didn't offer them any help, nor did any organizations for the wounded. Muhannad's condition is still precarious. The family is trying to save him from being disabled for life.

MY BROTHER'S SOUL DIDN'T SURVIVE

The wind outside won't stop whistling in my ears. Our usha shakes; I flinch. No one lives here except for me, my father, my younger brother, the palm trees and this hut putting up a fight against the wind and the cold. Sometimes we sit facing one another and smile, as if the rest of our loved ones are still beside us. Other times we realize they were killed a while ago and here in the darkness all that remains are our heads bowed in grief. We close our eyes and sink into silence.

But like this wind that has been raging against the palm fronds of our usha for months, grief never subsides. Grief eats at our tired souls, grief is watchful like my father's eyes fixed on the door, waiting for my mother and siblings to return. Grief is lifeless like my wife and my son. Grief is speechless like my brother's silence.

Their faces and voices haunt me constantly. I remember that morning. It was half past six and as usual I was still in bed. There was no backbreaking work requiring us to get up early, so we remained stretched out till the weather improved. I remember my wife and my son that morning, how they tiptoed out so as not to wake me. I caught their steps, but wasn't yet fully awake. It was time for breakfast, so my wife, mother and sisters gathered in the shared kitchen. The kitchen was outside, right between my hut and my father's. I heard my younger siblings playing with my son, and sank deeper into lethargy.

I didn't hear the plane approaching, but the explosion jolted me awake. Palm fronds fell on my head. The room was full of dust. Terrified, I ran outside, but the dust blocked everything from view.

My brother Ali was standing at the door. I asked him about my wife, son and our other siblings; where did they go, had he seen them? But he didn't answer. I ran towards my father. Slowly the dust started to settle, clearing up a little. My brother Mohammed was sobbing, his intestines spilling out of his stomach. I still believed then that Mohammed was the only one who had been injured, and that the rest were probably hiding behind the palm trees.

We searched in the desert and behind the palms. We hoped to find them safe and sound. A long time passed as we looked and called out their names. But no sound came from behind the trees, nor from the vast desert behind us.

Once the dust had settled completely, we found them. Sprawled out, motionless in the sand where our kitchen had once been. Their blood mixed with the soil that covered their faces and mangled bodies. My young son Ahmad's body had been ripped in half. Some bodies had been thrown behind the shack, others had been flung by the rocket into a hole. And next to it, my brother rooted to the spot, staring into its depths.

Ali Jamai Mushasha

At 6.00 a.m. on Thursday, 12 January 2017, an Arab Coalition aircraft targeted the outdoor kitchen of Ali Jamai Mushasha's family in the al-Jah district of the al-Hudaydah governorate. His mother Saeeda Ibrahim Habl (35 years old), siblings Libya Jamii Mushasha (16 years old), Ikhlas Jamaii Mushasha (12 years old), Abdllah Jamai Mushasha (14 years old) and Mohammed Jamii Mushasha (10 years old) were all killed. His wife Saeeda Yahya Muhmari (20 years old) was also killed, along with his son Ahmad Ali Jamaii Mushasha (2 years old).

IT IS US WHO LOST OUR MEN

War came to a standstill in Aden, and I told myself we'd return to our home and be sheltered from the elements by our own four walls. I remember how happy we were, my children and I, as we travelled the path back. But when I opened the front door, I cried as if my husband had been killed all over again. They'd ransacked everything, leaving nothing. [*She cries.*] No one in the area of Hujayf has gone through what we have.[33] No one else has tasted bitterness, displacement, and humiliation like us. No family has been crushed by the war like ours. At first, we lived through some hard times because of the blockade imposed by the militia in our area. We couldn't find food to eat nearby. My husband and children would walk long distances to bring food back from areas like al-Shaikh Uthman or al-Mansoura. Sometimes they even took the boat to al-Buriqa. Despite the bitterness of those days, we were comforted by people's sincerity, kindness, solidarity, and sympathy for us, their neighbours.

In the early days of the war, we were united by our fear of the militia. Our children and husbands joined the Southern Resistance, and families didn't differentiate us from their other neighbours. My husband, sons, and all the other families in the Qahwaji neighbourhood joined the resistance, mostly made up of local residents and young men who wanted to defend the al-Tawahi area. They were all like brothers; one and the same. We opened our home to the resistance fighters, and would make them lunch and dinner. The women would work together in the kitchen, with every family bringing what was in their home, and others cooking it. But for my husband, who

33   An area that falls under the administration of the al-Tawahi district in the Aden governorate.

worked at the Balhaf shipping port, this wasn't enough. Instead, he went a step further. From a grocery shop one of our relatives owned, my husband would travel every day to the barricades in the mountains to supply the youth of the resistance with chilled water, juice and even cigarettes. They awaited him joyfully. He'd say, 'They're heroes, holed up there – we've got to support them.'

In the first days of May, our neighbourhood became a target of militia shelling. The shells fired from Suhban made our old houses shake. On 3 May the bombing intensified; we feared our house would fall on our heads at any moment. The militia were fiercely battling to bring al-'Tawahi's fall. At nine at night, just as we had finished preparing dinner for the resistance fighters, the first shell hit – right where they were about to eat. Our neighbour Abdelhakeem al-Shuwafi and another man from our neighbourhood were killed. My husband rushed out to assist the wounded. Another shell fell on those giving first aid, injuring my husband and killing four others. People said afterwards that an informant had shared the resistance fighters' location with the Houthis.

We didn't find out that day that my husband had been killed; it's just a wounded shoulder, people said. When the shelling intensified further, young men in our neighbourhood belonging to the resistance informed us we'd have to evacuate our home. One of them told us, 'Don't worry, you'll be back tomorrow.' At midnight we left our home, taking nothing with us; no money, no papers, no gold, just some fresh clothes for my wounded husband. When we quickly pulled the door shut behind us, we didn't know we wouldn't return for many months, and that our journey of displacement was only just beginning. A number of families in Hujayf fled their homes, finding shelter in schools and hospitals. Empty, locked houses were opened to shelter those on the run. It wasn't easy for any of them, but it was especially hard for us; we didn't find a place to lay our heads that night. Only at one in the morning did we reach my uncle's house. There, we learnt of my husband's death. My children fell apart. We hadn't been there long when a missile fell near the house and killed several passers-by. Again, the resistance fighters ordered us to vacate the house. [*She cries.*]

Where were we supposed to go in the middle of the night? There was no one to help us, and we had no money. I had no time to grieve my husband. But when the world shuts the door in your face, good people open another for you. The person who opened that door for us was Maha al-Sayed, my daughter's friend. I won't forget what she did for us as long as I live. She opened her home to us, and even bought us mattresses and blankets. We stayed in her house in al-Mansoura for one day before a shell hit her home and we were forced to go on the run again. At five in the morning, dogs were barking all around us, shells raining down on the area. We found shelter in another house, but we weren't alone. We were one of four families who had also fled al-Tawahi, a total of thirty-seven of us in the house. We sat there and waited. As soon as the sun rose, my sons set out to find an empty apartment, but they couldn't find one. We didn't have any chance of survival in Aden, so we decided to go to relatives in al-Rahida.[34]

We didn't have the money to travel; all I had was the wedding ring on my finger. I sold it and rented a minibus to drive to al-Rahida. When we got there, the sun was already setting. We thought our family and relatives would stand by us in our homelessness, but not a single one came to help. Family that we had opened our home

34 An area falling under the administration of the Khadeer
    district in the Taiz governorate.

to in Aden, people we didn't hesitate to help; they didn't even bother asking how we were. Most of our family were Mutahouthi,[35] and because we'd supported the resistance, they washed their hands of us.

I will never forget our horrific months in al-Rahida. We occupied a clinic in a village in inner Ma'rib. The militia bombed the village day and night. I remember the hospital's cold tiles, how alone we were, no clothes, no furniture, no water, no electricity. My son and daughter fetched water from the well. We had no oven, not even a stove. My son and daughter were forced to gather wood from the mountains day after day. All we ate was bread and tea; we stayed like this for four months. We've seen such miserable days, I tell you, humiliating days. [*She cries.*] Muna, my eldest daughter, just sleeps all the time. She refuses to face reality. Muna, who used to work in television in Aden, found herself forced to collect firewood from the mountains. No one asks about us; not our friends, our family, no one from the resistance, they've all abandoned us. General Ali Nasser Hadi,[36] that kind man, was the only one who cared what happened to us after we had to leave for al-Mansoura. He told Muna, 'We won't abandon you and your family, how could we? Your father died for us!' [*She cries.*] He wasn't like his brother, President Abdrabbuh Mansur Hadi, who brought the Houthi to Aden, and then ran away. Look at us now, we've been through so much. We who have suffered, been scattered, and lost our men, see how they're treating us.

Everything has changed; the resistance isn't what it was

35 A local term akin to 'Houthified', given to someone who grows to support the Houthi party.
36 Commander of the Fourth district, brother to the Yemeni president, Abdrabbuh Mansur Hadi. Hadi was killed on 6 May 2015, when the Houthi-Saleh militia stormed the al-Tawahi area in Aden.

in the early days of the war, when the best of the city's men joined ranks. Most of the honourable ones were killed at the start of the conflict. Now all that is left are turf wars. They deny my husband was ever in the resistance, and spend money compensating the families of the Southern martyrs, but nothing for us. They claim my husband was a 'Northerner', that he's originally from Taiz, even though he was born and bred in Aden. They denied he died a martyr in the ranks of the resistance. They said he died of fever, refusing our right to aid. A kilo of meat on Eid was all we ever got from the Emirates. Once, during Ramadan, my son went to the aid distribution office, where the lady in charge there, Zahra Saleh,[37] refused to give us anything. She said, 'The families of Hujayf are Northerners, they don't deserve anything.'

The war is horrifying, and our day-to-day remains the same. Hatred, segregation, rejection. I don't want anything from them – what my husband and sons did to resist the militia was for the sake of the city, I don't need any favours from anyone. Everything is now out in the open: the war and displacement showed us even family and friends can reject you. I suffer from asthma now. I can't stop thinking about those dark days, how everyone rejected us, we who lost our men. [*She cries.*]

Lul Sayf

On Sunday, 3 May 2015, the Houthi-Saleh militia targeted the Qahwaji neighbourhood of Hujayf in the district of al-Tawahi, Aden governorate. Two civilians were killed, and her husband was wounded. The next day, he died as a result of

37 A Yemeni activist, who belongs to the separatist Southern Movement calling for the independence of South Yemen from the north of the country.

his injuries, and here the ordeal of Lul and her family began, with homelessness and displacement from Aden to the area of al-Rahida in Taiz.

THE APACHE ISN'T LOOKING FOR FISH

I don't want to remember. I'm tired.

[*Bekhit falls silent, staring at the paint peeling from the ceiling, his feet sticking out from under the hospital bedsheet. His friends try to cheer him up with jokes, but he simply glares at everything around him. 'Don't hold it against him,' one of his friends says. 'He went through a lot to save the others.' Bekhit catches our conversation and starts talking.*]

Our boat was the first to be hit that night. We watched as the light of an Apache helicopter lit up the black night sky and the sea surrounding us. We hadn't heard it approach; it might as well have fallen out of the sky. We were alarmed, but soon returned to work. It never crossed our minds the helicopter would attack us. We assumed it'd just happened to pass over on its way somewhere else. Nothing worth targeting here, just a bunch of fishermen eking out a living. But we didn't have much time to think. The Apache started firing at our boat at seven in the evening, after we'd set off from the coast of al-Hudaydah at one that afternoon. We'd already reached al-Sandal, where we always fish. It's a calm and quiet area; no military bases or armed fighters, just fishing boats. When the Apache started firing, we tried to dodge the bullets and shield our heads, but there was nothing in our small boat to shelter under.

How can I forget the Apache attacking us, trapped in a boat in the middle of the sea? No matter how loud we screamed, there was no one to save us; no other fishing boats, just darkness and water. We fell; some injured, some dead. Not a sound came from us – no one dared breathe. Once the helicopter had made sure no movement was coming from our boat, it disappeared as suddenly as it had arrived. [*A nurse comes into the room and interrupts Bekhit's recollections. 'Will you photograph Bekhit? If so, let me just change the sheets.' I shake my head, no. Bekhit continues.*]

Only when I opened my eyes did I realize I too was wounded. My friends lay still. I tried to get up, but could hardly move. I mustered all my strength and went to check on my friends. Two of them, Abdallah Daboush and Abdallah Ali Jaber, were dead, their bodies full of holes thanks to the Apache. Their blood was all over the boat. [*His voice catches and he falls silent.*]

I felt around for the rest of my friends, who were lying wounded, unconscious. I searched the boat for something to stop the bleeding; when I couldn't find anything, I lost all hope of survival. Sometime later, I tried again to find something to cover the bleeding. I poured whatever concentration, strength and energy I had left into saving my remaining friends. Despite my injuries, I was still conscious. Where I got the strength and perseverance remains a mystery. When I think back to that ordeal, I feel like I was another person; one who could only see his friends' pain, wanting to save them at all costs. But how could we survive when we were all so badly wounded? There was nothing in the bullet-riddled boat to bandage up our wounds. Water was streaming in. I remember looking around and contemplating our imminent death. I went in circles trying to find something, anything, to save us from drowning. I finally managed to tie my injured friends together by their legs. I bound them and then myself securely. Then I lay down next to the corpses of my two friends.

We are all from the village of al-Sabari,[38] and know each other well. We're more like family than friends. I lost two of them that day. We always used to go to that

38   A village in the governorate of al-Hudaydah.

area; we'd been there ever since we became fishermen. It's about sixteen kilometres from al-Tarfah Island. It'd always been safe. We'd never heard of any Coalition helicopters attacking boats and killing those aboard so mercilessly. If we'd heard of such a thing, we wouldn't have gone out to sea. What had my friends ever done to deserve this – why were they killed? [*He falls silent.*]

Our boat, torn into by the Apache gunfire, was drifting across the sea. I didn't care where we ended up; we were all wounded and awaiting our inevitable fate. Twenty-two hours had passed since the Apache attack, and we were still at sea. When another fishing boat passed by it was Jalba,[39] about five the next afternoon. The fishermen rescued us and pulled our boat ashore, where we were taken to hospital.

Twenty-two hours we were stuck at sea, wounded and exhausted. Long, sad, dark hours. What was it like for me? What did I feel? I don't ever want to remember.

Bekhit Ahmad Abdullah

At 7.00 p.m. on Wednesday, 15 March 2017, a Saudi Apache helicopter attacked a fishing boat. Bekhit Ahmad Abdullah, Esaam Muafi, Hamdi Sayyed, Mohammed Rabeed, and Hasan Jaadar were wounded. Bekhit's friends Abdallah Ali Jaber and Abdallah Daboush Musa Jamal were killed. I visited Bekhit in the al-Aqsa hospital in the al-Hudaydah governorate.

---

39   A term used by fishermen for the time they set out for sea and start fishing.

SALLY, WHERE'S YOUR SISTER?

My sister Sara and I, we did everything together. Too much for me to count. Sometimes we'd scrub the walls of our house on holidays while my mother and other sisters baked cake and sweets. We'd dust off the windows, singing at the top of our lungs like two naughty children who'd never grown up.

Sometimes we set what we'd learnt at school to the tune of one of our favourite songs, bopping our heads along and laughing. We were always together, doing everything together: choosing our outfits together – they had to be matching – sleeping in the same room, the same bed. We went to university together, studied in the same department, had the same friends.

One dawn, the dog barked, but my mother didn't hear him. His cries grew louder in the darkness. Awake, we opened the window, and he started to bark even louder. He was lying on the hill across from our house. That day, our friend who was staying with us after fleeing her own home said, 'When a dog barks like that, someone, somewhere is about to die.' I didn't pay much attention to her words, but the dog's howls continued, stirring up dread and making me think of Sara.

I remember standing on the balcony that day. We were looking out at the city's alleyways. There was a fresh breeze that we soaked up. We smiled at each other. We heard the thunder of the shells, and contemplated the death all around us, but didn't let ourselves drown in sad thoughts. When we craned our necks over the railing, our building shook from a shell that had fallen elsewhere in our neighbourhood. We saw men running panicked into nearby buildings. When we were sure no one was hurt, we sat by the balcony door again. We were laughing at something or other, I don't remember what now. Sara wiggled her eyebrows at me in that endearing way of hers whenever she described something and her words failed her – I laughed.

The thunder of the shell deafened me. I couldn't hear a thing. The room filled with dust and a sharp pain shot through my little finger. I ran out of the room, and my siblings encircled me. My brother assured me my finger was still in one piece. My mother then asked, 'Sally, where's your sister?' I just remember running, and running to our room, but never getting there. As I ran, our room, with my sister inside, grew further and further away – I couldn't reach her. Out of breath, I stopped. Sara was sitting very still, leaning slightly to the side, just how I had left her: a faint smile on her lips like she still had something to say. She sat in a small pool of blood. I shook Sara's head violently, but she didn't answer. I called her name. Nothing.

I cried. She wasn't answering me. [*She cries.*]

At sunset the militia murdered my sister Sara. I couldn't go out into the world without her there. It's not so much the memories of her that pain me, it's more complicated than that. I feel I only lived my life through her, and she lived hers through me. It's as if life has been cut out of me. I envy those who can flee their memories and free themselves from such a pain. In the beginning, I wanted to change university, department and subject altogether. I couldn't face the everyday reminder of her absence. I remember my first day back at university after Sara's death, months later. I was on the bus, looking at the reflection of faces and roads on the glass. I remembered how Sara had always sat next to me, and cried. Friends chatting, their laughter, the wind in the al-Habeel university trees, how we'd stand around, climbing the stairs to the professors' rooms, their confusion over who was who, the footsteps of hardworking students on their way to lectures, the fountain gurgling, the man selling textbooks at the kiosk, the cafeteria worker, the sounds of daily life flowing – everything reminded me of Sara.

None of our family has forgotten Sara; she's unforgettable. Everyone mourns her, whether at home or university. My mother cries all the time. On dark nights I hear her sobbing alone, her voice catching when she's kneeling to pray, or muttering in her sleep. In those moments, I know she's thinking of Sara. But I can't bear to think of how Sara isn't with us any more. I refuse to give her clothes away, or remove her photos from our bedroom walls. I've left our bedroom just as it was and keep on sharing the bed with her, our things, memories, and stories. When I miss her, I look at photos of us together, and forbid anyone to erase her from this world.

My memories with Sara are always there. A voice in my head repeats, 'Sally, where's your sister?'

'The war took her, Umma.'

Sally Hasan Hizaa Salah

At 5.15 p.m. on Saturday, 19 September 2015, the Houthi-Saleh militia shelled the al-Hazami grocery shop in al-Masbah al-Asfal in Taiz. Sally's sister Sara Hasan Hizaa Salah was killed (22 years old).

NO ONE WANTS TO KNOW WHAT HAPPENED TO US

You never know when they'll come for you. You could be at home, getting ready for bed, playing with your children – when all of a sudden there's a knock at the door. You could be walking down the street alone, or even chatting away with friends, then you disappear. You never know when they'll come, but they always know. You've no idea what they'll claim you've done, or why they'll take you away. I had no idea why they took me.

I'd just bought dinner for my family, as I always did after work, and was walking down one of the alleyways by my home. It was nine at night. I don't remember the date. All I remember is turning my head to see a van stopped beside me. I can't recall the model, or what my kidnappers looked like, but I know there were five of them, all armed. All I saw of the driver were his two fingers nervously dangling a lit cigarette out the window. They shoved me into the vehicle. I didn't fight back. I don't remember anything after that. My eyes opened when the car stopped in front of the prison.

They accused me of being a soldier for the official government. 'But, I'm not a soldier,' I told them. 'I'm a salesman, I have nothing to do with the war.' But they didn't believe me. Each day another interrogation; each day I repeated the same answers. Once they'd had enough of my screams, they said, 'You'll confess all right, no matter what it takes...' Depriving me of humanity was their next tactic. In those moments, your body confesses against your will. But my body resisted; it defied the torture, refusing to confess to a crime I didn't commit. My body persevered through those months. They hung me from the ceiling. I stared at their shoes as they whipped me. With every lash they yelled, 'Confess!' I'd tell the truth and they'd grow more enraged, torturing me even more. At some point they'd leave my lifeless body alone.

We measured time by the pain and torture our bodies endured, the hunger and obsessive thoughts that drained us. Every part of my body groaned. I would curl into a ball to sleep, but sleep never came. I'd think of my family and wonder what would come of me in prison. Then I'd hear shrieks of pain coming from what used to be the women's wing, and what little chance of sleep I'd had faded away. We'd bow our heads in fear, forgetting our own ordeals and why we were kidnapped. They were prisoners like us, but they were called Dawaesh.[10] Who knows how many there were. We weren't allowed to mix with them; they were held at a distance. Only sometimes, would our eyes meet through the bars.

I've forgotten most of my cellmates' names, but I remember their faces and harrowing tales. One had been arrested a few months before me, for delivering goods from al-Hudaydah to the Saudi Arabian border. His family had no idea he had been taken. Another was a jasmine flower seller at Mushrif Gate; arrested simply because they thought he looked suspicious. Another's face was burnt during interrogations. He said the neighbourhood elder had sold him out, telling them he'd sided with the enemy. Most of our stories were similar; we'd all been brought in on false charges. In al-Zaydiyya prison,[41] we were removed from the world; no one asked about us, no family, no friends. I often used to think of my family;

40   This term is used to describe those associated with the Islamic State. The Houthi-Saleh militia use it to label anyone who thinks differently politically in order to have a reason to imprison them.
41   Al-Zaydiyya prison is located in the district of al-Zaydiyya, governorate of al-Hudaydah.

four months passed and they still had no idea where I was. I'd gone out one night to buy dinner, never to return. Did they eat that evening or fall asleep hungry? Such thoughts kept me up at night – then everything changed.

It was nine o'clock at night. We were ready to sleep when we heard the first explosion. We yelled, pleading with the jailers to open the cell doors so we wouldn't burn alive. I still remember the sobs of a friend, 'For God's sake, open the door!' And when the second missile hit, we all fainted. A lot of my friends suffered burns, and I was wounded by shrapnel. On that night, sixty prisoners in the women's wing were hit by a Coalition missile. They took us to the hospital, and all I remember are the police and observers[42] walking between us. That day, the freezer in the morgue stopped working because there was no more diesel. The burnt bodies were gathered in a truck; random hands mixed with random feet. Families couldn't identify their loved ones. [*He cries.*]

I still remember what Yassin Taher Ahmad's father said. We never found out why Yassin was arrested. His father learnt about the missile attack when he was told his son had burned to death in prison. The father didn't cry, he simply took his son's body to bury him safely in the village. But they hadn't let him keep his son's body. Due to a mistake by one of the hospital officers, the body of a Houthi military commander, killed on the frontlines, was placed in the same freezer as the dead from the women's wing. So one day the Houthi fighters came to Yassin's father's door to reclaim the body he'd thought was his son's. They dug the corpse from the grave before his weeping father, who'd now lost his son a second time.

---

42 People belonging to the Houthi movement, who are placed in every state institution of the country. Their powers in the areas under Houthi authority are increasing.

What happened in al-Zaydiyya prison stays in al-Zaydiyya prison. No one knows what was done to us. We, who watched our fellow inmates burn, are the only ones who know. We were unfairly detained, spending our days between torture, starvation and sickness, until finally the Coalition planes brought an even unhappier ending to so many of us.

One of the injured from al-Zaydiyya prison

At 9.00 p.m. on Saturday, 29 October 2016, Arab Coalition planes shot two rockets at al-Zaydiyya prison. Fifty-nine inmates were killed, the majority of whom had been arrested for political reasons by the Houthi party. During identification of the burnt corpses, marks of torture were evident. After the bombing, the Houthi party tried to hide the existence of the prison, just as the Arab Coalition had. Out of fear for his life, the narrator of this account chose to remain anonymous.

YOU WOULD HAVE LOVED MY MOTHER

It's been three months since I left al-Jumhuri. I remember our life there, in that old neighbourhood in Taiz, a happy family, our mother at the centre. After our father died when we were young, she became our everything. But when war came to the city, our lives changed. Our neighbourhood became the frontline of war and hatred – the militia dropped missiles on us from al-Silal hill, the Sofitel hotel, or the General People's Congress Party headquarters.[43] The resistance, concentrated in the saila,[44] fired back, lighting up the sky of our neighbourhood and sometimes dropping missiles on nearby houses. As if the fighters – as my aunt would say – were telling the missiles, 'God's speed, wherever you may fall.'

My mother didn't like the idea of leaving, but after a shell fell on our home and destroyed the bathroom walls, she agreed to move to her sister's temporarily. We stayed a few months before a missile fell there too, burning the house to the ground. That day, my mother insisted we go back home. 'Listen children, I'm tired of being on the run. We'll just stay in our own home, come what may.' Missiles hit our neighbourhood once more, and we huddled round my mother, frightened. With my mother, we were strong; with her around, there was a reassuring presence in the house. The missiles came; we hid in the living room, the only safe place in the house. My siblings and I collected there, waiting for the bombing to stop. We didn't have a basement like others did. The war wouldn't leave us alone; it chased us and took what we cherished most.

---

43 Located on a hill in the middle of the governorate of Taiz, the militia have occupied these headquarters and use it as a launch pad to shoot missiles at civilians.
44 A fortified riverbed in which rain collects during certain seasons.

That dawn, our lives changed forever. We were never the same, now homeless. [*She cries.*]

We were all up late that night. My aunt Karima and her daughters were staying with us after their house was destroyed, burnt to ashes by a missile. My mother was happy to have her sister nearby. I can see my mother now, in her red dressing gown, embroidered with grey roses. The house was full and they were all laughing heartily. I left their company and went to my room, chuckling at the echoes of their laughter from the living room. I don't know when exactly the laughter became screams and wailing. No matter how hard I try, I can't remember. Maybe it was at two thirty in the morning. I heard my aunt and her daughters wailing, and my brother Ammar scream. Terrified, I ran to find my mother swimming in her own blood, part of her head on the wall opposite. My aunt and her daughters kept crying. As did my brother Ammar, while he tried to piece together my mother's brains. 'They're still soft, Nabila,' he said. [*She cries.*]

I remember looking out the window at the dark night, yelling and yelling for someone to save my mother. Barking dogs were the only response. My brother Rabeea ran to the lower part of the neighbourhood, looking for a taxi or bus to take my mother to hospital, but there was no one to save her. All the neighbours were afraid another missile would drop and had gone into hiding. There was nothing in those alleyways except for dogs barking; they smelt the blood on my brother's clothes.

The militia murdered my mother with a modified machine gun. It was shot from the General People's Congress Party headquarters. The bullet pierced our wall, then the cupboard facing it, then the pillows, finally entering my mother's head. They murdered my mother, the beauty of our souls and our greatest support in this life. So we left the neighbourhood and the city altogether, to live with our aunt Jameela in Sanaa.

I think of our neighbourhood all the time, of life there with our mother. Are you familiar with al-Jumhuri? Have your feet ever carried you there, or have you strolled through the alleyways of the old city and headed north? Or maybe on your way to the hospital at the end of the street? That's our neighbourhood: travelling salesmen hawking gas canisters and potatoes. Turning left you would have seen our small house looking out over the back alleys, the twists of the paths, rowdy neighbourhood children playing football, pushing one another noisily, racing each other to the ice cream seller's cart. Maybe you also would have heard my mother's voice resounding in the afternoon, calling out for my brother Ammar. You would have loved her sweet voice. You would have loved her, just as we love and miss her now. [*She cries.*] Maybe you would have heard her sewing machine rattling away during the stagnant nights, as she expertly made dresses for our neighbours with doting hands – all to provide for us after my father's death. You would have loved this woman who fought for the sake of her children. You would have worried, hearing her wheezing cough as she complained of the ache in her heart.

Now my mother is no longer in this world, our al-Jumhuri is no longer what it once was. The militia killed my mother; now me and my younger brother are in another city, orphans. But I always think of our old neighbourhood left in ruins by the war. I grieve over how life used to be when we had a mother. When we still had a life.

Nabila Abdelkareem Ahmad Farhaan

At 2.30 a.m. on Wednesday, 2 March 2016, Houthi-Saleh

militia bombed the family's house in al-Jumhuri neighbour-
hood in Taiz with a modified machine gun bullet. Nabila's
mother Samira al-Dailami was killed.

THEY STOLE MY JOY

I'd barely been married two months when everything came to an end. Before, my life had been a dream, everything bright. Lights above our heads, decorations hanging in every corner of the house, my cousin Ghala, the love of my life in her white dress and veil. Trills of joy burst from the women's mouths, our family gathered in the courtyard of the house, my own heart melting with happiness. Everything was shining: the floor, the walls, and my eyes that saw the world as beautiful. Everything was as bright and pure as I felt inside. My mother embraced us, congratulating us on our marriage. Ghala and I strolled hand in hand down the rose-decorated corridor, like two children, excited for the life that awaited us. The whole family was there: my sister laughing, my sister-in-law rocking her youngest son to the beat of the music, my brother dancing and grinning, then it all disappeared.

I remember the sunset that day. My wife had gone to my cousin's next door. The women in the family had gathered there to celebrate my wife, who was still a newlywed according to our village customs. She left our house, a bride once more, but the next time I saw her was as a charred corpse. I was in the souk, just a few metres from our home; the hustle and bustle of the neighbours earning their daily bread enveloped me. A plane had been flying up ahead since four o'clock in the afternoon; I assumed it was on its way somewhere else. I mean, what business would a plane have in such an out-of-the-way place? There aren't any militia or barracks here, just the scattered houses and huts of the villagers. Mid-thought, I heard the blast of the missile. It was five-thirty in the afternoon. I thought the missile must have fallen far away, that they must have been aiming for some patrol,

131

barracks or fighters stationed somewhere, or any place they considered worth bombing the enemy and wiping them out completely. It didn't occur to me that the missile would find only my cousin's house in its path, killing all the women and children inside.

I saw smoke rising from the house. My knees gave out and I sank to the ground. Once I regained my strength, I ran along with everyone else flocking to the site of the explosion. The house had collapsed; the walls now crushing my family's skulls. [*He falls silent.*] I couldn't make out who was who. All the bodies were jumbled up, their clothes burnt, making them seem naked. I sobbed as I turned over the piled-up bodies. I tried to find my wife and the rest of my family. The bodies were in pieces, hands on one side, heads on the other. A human barbecue.

Later, I identified my wife Ghala, my sister Rahab, and my brother Nadir. I let my gaze travel and on the other side saw my sister-in-law Uhud and her youngest son Mohammed. I cried in disbelief. My brother cried for his wife and four children. Our neighbour cried for his wife and three sons. All of them were dead. My eyes moved over the corpses, my brother cradling the remains of his wife and children. His sobs choked me. I tried to calm him down, but my mother's wailing for her children drowned me out. [*He cries.*]

Our life as bright as a dream; they took it from us. All that's left is bitterness. The Coalition murdered my family, my brother's family and my neighbour's family. What had these innocents ever done? Why were women and children killed in cold blood? They weren't fighters, and had nothing to do with this war. This is what I ask when I take a look at my life now. I can't believe what happened. All that's left of my family are my father, my mother, and two of my siblings who happened to be out of the house when the missile hit. My nephew Akram is still injured, and can no longer walk. No one cares about us, no organizations, no government agencies – to them we aren't even human. We don't deserve their sympathy.

Do you think we'll ever forget? How can I forget the murder of my wife, my siblings, my brother's family? We'd barely been married two months when they stole my joy. [*He turns to the remains of the destroyed house and falls silent.*]

Rahib Abdelkarim Abdelhamid

At 5.40 p.m. on Thursday, 26 January 2017, Arab Coalition planes bombed Rahib's neighbour Fahmi Abdelhamid Sayf's house, in the al-Qutay area of the al-Hudaydah governorate. Rahib's wife Ghala Mohammed Abdelhamid Huzaa was killed (18 years old), as well as his sister Rahab Abdelkarim Abdelhamid (16 years old), brother Nadir Abdelkarim Abdelhamid (11 years old), sister-in-law Uhud Khaled Salem Mohammed (26 years old) and her son Mohammed Rafat Abdelkarim Abdelhamid (eighteen months old). Four others from the neighbour's family were also killed in the bombing.

DEATH BY DECEPTION

There wasn't a sound outside; life was seemingly muted during that Ramadan. It was ten in the morning, or maybe eleven, I don't know exactly. What I remember of that day is silence and the light that flooded the city, illuminating Yusuf's face, my sweet nephew, who we named in remembrance of my father. Yusuf was getting ready to leave the house. I asked him, 'Where you going at this hour? It's Ramadan after all, and everyone is still asleep.' He responded, his voice apologetic, 'I'll just see what my friends want. Don't worry, I'll be right back.' I remember his final affectionate gesture. Whenever I think of this moment, my heart breaks. [*She cries.*]

The war forced our children to pick up guns, to leave their schoolbooks and work behind. They carried weapons to take on the militia. We'd see them sometimes at their posts on the frontlines near the city, gaunt and exhausted. They'd been excited about their decision, but we never discussed it. When we looked into their vigilant eyes, we prayed for their survival. One day, my son Amjad joined the resistance, too. He didn't tell anyone, but I sensed it when he'd go missing day and night for hours on end, as well as from his tales of friends' resilience at the front and the barricades. We knew they were far from us; our hearts bled whenever we thought of one of them risking their lives. But Yusuf, my nephew, he was different from the other young men that joined. He was shy; he didn't brag like the others. He didn't talk about the resistance, and we only learned of his life behind the barricades when it was already too late.

When Yusuf's reputation as a resistance fighter made the rounds in town, his father asked him about it. When I think back to their conversation, I cry. His father had been waiting for him to come back that night. 'Son, everyone's saying you climbed the Maqrami building on 26 September Street with men from the resistance?'

'Ya'ba don't believe everything you hear,' Yusuf had said. He didn't want to alarm his father. He'd kept joining the resistance a secret, and didn't want glory or money. After his murder, we learnt that Yusuf hadn't put his real name on the register, but an alias that he liked to be called by: 'al-Sudani'. Every day, the city paid final respects to new corpses from the resistance killed on the front lines, while we mourned. But Yusuf wasn't killed in battle; he was killed by deception.

The Houthis deceived Yusuf. They didn't kill him like a man, face to face, or take aim at him on the frontlines of war. They tailed him for some time. And one fateful day, they set a trap for him. Disguised as resistance fighters, they waited outside our house. They called out for al-Sudani, as if they were close friends. Yusuf went out with them calmly, unaware of their plans until they lured him into a building and locked the door. Yusuf tried to fight them, but he was unarmed. For days the Houthis tortured him, mutilating his body, before executing him by gunfire and hanging him. They tied him up with wire, wrapped him up in a blanket, and let him hang for days. Then they threw him in Qasim's yard. [*She cries.*]

We searched for Yusuf everywhere: the streets, hospitals, prisons. No trace. Hammoud Said[45] remarked that day, 'If al-Sudani is being held hostage, I'll exchange twenty Houthis for him. He's irreplaceable.' We left no stone unturned, but there was no sign of him. For days we didn't sleep, my girl, and couldn't sit still. We didn't pay attention to the screams of the neighbourhood madman

45   A leader belonging to the Yemeni Islah party, and of the popular resistance in the governorate of Taiz.

that used to pass by Qasim's yard, yelling, 'Here lies al-Sudani! Here lies al-Sudani!' We didn't believe him, and once we were tired of searching, young men from the resistance went to that yard and found Yususf's body. My son Amjad identified him from his T-shirt. He said, 'That's him.'

Yusuf's body had scars all over. His eyes were swollen. They brutally tortured him. They made such an example of him that he was unrecognizable. [*She cries.*]

Fatima Mohammed Yusuf

On Monday, 6 July 2015, the Houthi-Saleh militia in Wadi al-Madam, governorate of Taiz, killed her nephew Yusuf Ahmad Mohammed Yusuf (29 years old), and made an example of his body.

NO LONGER OUR CITY

In an old nightmare of mine, Abdelhabib never appears. A black stream gushes forth from somewhere in the al-Jahmiliya neighbourhood;[46] I don't know where that filthy dark water comes from. Grimy black water, with no beginning or end, pouring out from behind the mud houses, the mosques, and the old shops. Houses and people disappear in the current's path as it makes its way through the city and veils the sky; a city, drowning. For three months before the war began, I had the same nightmare over and over. Once it started, I realized the black current was the war itself, that it would sweep us away and destroy our lives.

Before the black tide of war, we lived in peace in our house next to the Taiz police department. We were born in these old mud houses, just like our grandparents and parents before us. Here in Taiz, we went to school and later on to university. We grew up, got married, and lived in peace, like the rest of the city's inhabitants. We love this city and the kind people who live here. The thought never crossed our minds that life here would change, and that a day would come where our ancestry became a reason for us to be arrested, killed and wiped out. I never thought that we, the people who grew up in this city, would simply become the strangers from Anis.[47]

The families with whom we had shared our lives and memories, joys and sorrows, now looked at us fearfully

---

46   One of the oldest neighbourhoods in the city of Taiz. Due to the war, clashes here are sectarian in nature – some of the neighbourhood identify themselves as part of the Zaidi sect from the Shi'ite branch, and the remaining count themselves among the al-Shafiee sect of the Sunni school of law.
47   Neighbourhood in the city of Dhamar, in the south-west of Yemen, 160 kilometres north-east of Taiz.

and informed on us to the authorities. I don't know how the delicate bond of co-existence and love was broken. Today we are hated. We who had no ill will towards them. The more the war raged in the city, the more we feared for our lives. The neighbourhood residents passed on news that the Coalition would soon bomb the police department. And so we were forced to leave our home and the city, in which we'd been born and raised, for Sanaa. We told ourselves we'd be back once the war was over. Abdelhabib, though, insisted on staying back in the house. 'This is my city,' he said. 'These are my people. Nothing's going to happen to me.' [*She cries.*]

I still remember those days in August, the sound of shelling echoing throughout every corner of the city. After driving the militia from the area, the resistance occupied the police department. Residents were joyful, thinking the resistance would make the area secure. But instead, the resistance arrested many of the neighbourhood's people; innocents who had nothing to do with war or politics. Innocent people slandered with various accusations by their neighbours. Since then, those arrested have disappeared, their families never hearing from them again. One day, we heard al-Qaeda members, led by al-Harith al-Azee,[48] had stormed our home. Abdelhabib was still asleep inside. Neighbours also informed us that Abdelhabib had been kidnapped by Emad al-Sanaani[49] and Ali al-Dubaii.[50] Or that Ali al-Dubaii had shot Abdelhabib in the police headquarters. Yes, they say they saw him that morning, shooting at Abdelhabib until he bled to death. They told us the person who'd condemned Abdelhabib was his half-brother, who'd been recruited

48   An al-Qaeda leader in the Taiz governorate.
49   Another al-Qaeda leader in the Taiz governorate.
50   An al-Qaeda leader in the Taiz governorate killed on 27 September 2015.

by al-Qaeda years before. He told them that Abdelhabib doesn't pray. Abdelhabib doesn't fast. Abdelhabib is a kafir. They then kidnapped Abdelhabib and killed him for being a kafir. Our hearts cried out at what the neighbours described to us, at what they claimed to have seen with their own eyes. And yet, they refused to give a formal statement. They changed their phone numbers, afraid of us searching for the truth.

Others told us Abdelhabib was killed for his new Nissan. Some neighbours called us to say they'd seen al-Qaeda members driving Abdelhabib's Nissan in the city in broad daylight. It was as if they were telling us, 'Yes, we did it. We killed him, and stole his car. All right before your eyes, and you can't do anything about it.' Terrified, we kept our mouths shut. We were also told that Abdelhabib was killed because he'd been fighting the pro-government resistance, and waging war in the Houthi ranks. We laughed when we heard that one. What liars. Abdelhabib had been one of the Shabab al-Thawra, the revolutionary youth who had taken to the streets to oppose Saleh. And when the war started, he still stood against the Houthis and Saleh, but was against the religious organizations and parties that controlled the city. Abdelhabib was a peaceful man; he worked as a supervisor in the Ministry of Education. Not a single day in his life did he carry a weapon. Never held a grudge against anyone.

Some people told us Abdelhabib had been killed because his ancestors hailed from Dhamar, and that must've been why he was in cahoots with the Houthis. When we learnt of how they murdered Khalil al-Anisi[51] and threw his body in the dried-up riverbed, we were terrified.

---

51   Khalil al-Anisi's corpse was found on 28 June 2015 in the
      al-Saeed riverbed in the governorate of Taiz.

Our neighbour's whispers, their looks, how short they were with us, their condescending gestures, their wariness, saying we were Houthi and 'Sayyids',[52] this all made us believe the same had happened to Abdelhabib. Even though we hated the Houthis, and didn't identify as Sayyid. We have nothing to do with the Houthis or Saleh, but they still pigeonholed us to justify their hatred. We used to believe ourselves children of this city we love, and that our ancestry meant no one had the right to throw us out.

Others said they had witnessed Abdelhabib's murder. When we asked them about the corpse, they fell silent. They then said there was a body buried in the grounds of the police headquarters, and that it had to be Abdelhabib's. Others insisted we search the dry riverbed, where the resistance had killed opposing elements. Rain poured down the day Abdelhabib was killed, so it could well be that his body had been swept away by the water, they said. Someone told my grandmother he had seen Abdelhabib's head hanging somewhere in the old city. When we asked him to give a statement, he denied ever saying anything. My grandmother died grief-stricken over her nephew.

Where had they hidden Abdelhabib and why? What had Abdelhabib ever done for our hearts to be torn up over him like this? Did they kill him, or was he in a cellar somewhere? Sometimes we'd stare at the door rattling, telling ourselves, Abdelhabib's going to knock now, and we'll rejoice; just now, we'll hear his new car he bought a few months ago honking, and we'll go out to see him. He'll come in any minute now, telling us about his wedding date and all the preparations. But once we got tired of waiting, despair ate us up, and we thought of everything

52 Sayyids claim they can trace their genealogy back to the Prophet Mohammed.

people had told us. We didn't believe anything they had to say. We searched the prisons. When we didn't find him, we asked some neighbours to look for Abdelhabib's body once more in the dry riverbed – but they didn't find him.

Without a body, we couldn't believe they'd killed him. So many bodies only appeared long after they had been murdered. The old man who had been shot by the militia, his body was only found a year later on the roof of his house. Everyone who said they had seen Abdelhabib killed was afraid of going on record. We didn't reach out to the Red Cross or any other organization, terrified in case al-Qaeda might kill more of our family. Some good, well-meaning people warned us, 'Don't look for Abdelhabib, they're watching you.'

When we think of our beloved Abdelhabib, and how we don't know what happened to him, we feel powerless and humiliated. Did the extremists really kill him? And if so, why? Were they that blinded by their hatred? Our hands are tied. We never get any sleep. We're always crying over Abdelhabib, not knowing whether he's alive or dead. But our hearts will never believe he's dead unless we see his body with our own eyes, touch it with our own hands. When we think of this city, Taiz; our hearts hurt, we love it, but it's no longer ours.

A relative of Abdelhabib Mohammed al-Qadiri

On 19 August 2015, a faction of al-Qaeda, loyal to the resistance in the governorate of Taiz, kidnapped Abdelhabib Mohammed al-Qadiri (38 years old). To this day, his family have no knowledge of what happened to him, and have not reported him missing to any official agency. The witness of this account remains anonymous for fear of their life.

THIS IS THE APOCALYPSE, NOT WAR

At the al-Dehi checkpoint,[53] the soldiers' faces change just as their filthy uniforms do, but their weapons remain aimed at our heads. Their aggressive tone may change, the weather may change, but we women of this city never do. We, who are under siege, with nothing left at home to eat. We have to repeatedly risk crossing this death strip. There are women as far as the eye can see, some of them in lines, others in circles. Sometimes they stand in the street or sit on the pavement facing the crossing, protecting themselves from the sun with cardboard boxes over their heads. Next to them are empty gas cylinders and their young children.

At various times and places, I remember leaning on my cane, walking long distances on my exhausted feet, fear in my heart. But hunger forces me to take the risk. If the soldier was preoccupied, sometimes just by coincidence I could cross over to the market on the other side of the checkpoint. I'd buy what I needed and return safely home. Other times the soldier would forbid me to pass, and I'd stand next to the gate, my anger choking me.

One day during the blockade, the gas ran out at home once again. My daughters were worried, and forbade me from going to al-Dehi, but I went out behind their backs. Exhausted, I reached the crossing and tried to walk through, but the soldier blocked me. I swallowed my anger and stood to the side. Dozens of women were waiting, like me, to be let through. Looking at the crowds of women made my blood boil. Another day, I crossed the al-Dehi checkpoint and bought a sack of potatoes. By

53   In July 2015, Houthi-Saleh militia set up a military checkpoint in the al-Dehi area, west of the city of Taiz, and enforced a fatal blockade on the city's families.

chance that day a friendly young man said, 'Khala, I've got two gas cylinders here, but I'm sure the soldier won't let me bring them in. How about I push the shopping trolley for you and you add my cylinders to your sack?' I agreed, but when we reached the gate, the soldier blocked me, pulled a dagger from his belt and slit the potato sack open.[54] The potatoes rolled everywhere.

I remember a sad day at al-Dehi, when one of my daughters had insisted on accompanying me. The road to the checkpoint was full of women. I stood with the women, waiting for the soldier to let us pass. First the soldier shot into the air, and then he aimed his gun at the women's feet to stop them going any further. My daughter was among those women. As the women screamed, the taste of humiliation shot up from my stomach to my mouth. 'Why are you shooting at us? Do we look armed?' I protested. He barked, 'Taiz women are animals.' I then said, 'Taiz women will fight you where you stand, and twenty others like you.' He then yelled, 'What do you want old woman?' 'I want to buy food for my children.' 'Go on then,' he said. 'But I need my daughters, I'm sick and I can't carry everything.' I called out some names and many women ran towards me. The soldier blocked them. 'They're all your daughters?' I said, 'Shame on you, let them pass to buy their children food.'

We were risking our lives standing where we were, and if we backed down or turned away, they'd never let us cross again. On the way back, we faced another soldier; an even ruder, heartless man. He didn't respect my old age and screamed in my face, 'Go back old woman, you won't get through here.' 'Will you keep us at yours then?' I asked. There was a man from the Habashi Mountain area,

54   At the al-Dehi checkpoint, Houthi-Saleh militia wouldn't
      allow citizens to buy more than a kilo of vegetables.

a Houthi sympathizer, who said, 'Khala, don't play with fire, you'll get burned.' I responded, 'He can't touch me.' We walked a little further towards the gate. My daughter was afraid we'd get shot. I really was taking risks that day, the life-or-death kind of ones. At that time the price of a gas cylinder had reached 9000 riyals. We barely made it out. [*She laughs.*]

Another day, I went to al-Dehi, and their leader himself was there. They were calling him by his code name, Abu Ali;[55] a scary-looking man. I'll never forget his face. I heard later that a woman at the checkpoint had poisoned him. I also heard another story where he was found murdered. What we went through at the al-Dehi checkpoint, I can't put into words. One time, the militia arrested a young man who was just trying to buy food for his family. They beat him up and humiliated him in front of the women. Another man, an ice cream seller, was also beaten by a soldier in front of us, but the man didn't scream or cry out even once. He just kept staring into the soldier's eyes. My heart broke for this poor young man, and I told the soldier, 'Shame on you boy, why are you kicking him like this? He's human, just like you.' He growled, 'Move it before I stick this in your stomach.' He had his hand on his dagger.

One woman was with her son, who couldn't have been more than sixteen years old. He couldn't bear the way the soldier humiliated us women. When he cursed the soldier, he was dragged away to a shop. The militia had turned the shops at the al-Dehi crossing into prison cells, keeping young men locked up in there and torturing them. His mother threw herself to the ground, sobbing, kissing the soldier's boots. 'I beg you, he's all I have, take me instead,

55 Houthi militia always give their fighters code names to conceal their identity.

and let him go!' Another elderly woman argued with the soldier; he kicked her really hard and pushed her, and she rolled off the main road, crashing into a tree.

I can't even describe the humiliation we endured at that checkpoint; the soldiers' curses, their abuse. One day, I was walking with great difficulty, leaning heavily on my cane. A soldier joked, 'No trouble walking to Sanaa! Sluts.'[56] I answered him, 'We walked because we are brave.' Fear was always in al-Dehi, even after we passed the gate. We'd make our way to the souk, scared. We never used our phones, never picked up our family's calls. We'd walk with our heads lowered, afraid of the snipers hiding atop the buildings.

After the resistance liberated the al-Dehi area,[57] the bodies of soldiers and militia resistance fighters remained on the ground for days until they started to rot and stray dogs began to eat them. I didn't go to see their corpses. My daughter went with the rest of the spectators; she recognized the body of the soldier that had cursed and shot at us.

Whenever I pass by al-Dehi today, I avert my eyes so that I don't remember all we went through there. I've never seen anything like it, my girl. I'm now sixty years old; I've lived through the many wars that have come to this country, but none of them were like this. Back then, the fighters had morals at least, some sort of humanity. They didn't attack women, torture prisoners, or kill children. When the revolution broke out in the city of Taiz on 26 September 1962, my husband was one of the first to fight

56   The soldier was referring to the Taiz women's participation in the 'March for Life' (20–26 December 2011) from Taiz to Sanaa, a distance of 256 kilometres. The march took place as a protest against the regime of Ali Abdullah Salih. Bushra al-Maqtari was herself one of the leaders of this protest march.
57   The resistance liberated the al-Dehi crossing in March 2016.

against Imam Ahmad. When he was wounded in battle, he went on to join the National Guard in Sanaa, and fought there as well. But neither side committed massacres like this. All the terrors we have lived through in this war I can't even describe. This is the apocalypse, not war.

Khadija Mohammed Hassan

Khadija Mohammed Hassan played a significant role in breaking the blockade the Houthi-Saleh militia imposed on the city of Taiz, after a military checkpoint was erected in the area of al-Dehi. Khadija risked her life helping numerous others enter al-Dehi, and shared with them what she could bring from the souk. She talked of the blockade days with bitterness, about what the women there had faced, how they had been humiliated and degraded. I visited her at her home in Wadi al-Madam in Taiz. By candlelight she talked of the blockade days and the war, or the apocalypse, as she calls it.

ON THE EDGE OF A CRATER

Just like that, a three-storey home disappeared, leaving behind a crater in the ground. A meaningless hole; pedestrians rushing by pay it no attention. But for me, it's a hole full of eyes, memories and spirits. On the edges of this hole, lying beneath the rubble are pieces of warped furniture. You might see some family belongings: a photo of a little girl with her two brothers on her birthday, a tattered marriage certificate, a small, smashed toy, scattered clothes, squashed food, the juices running into the ground. Between the hole and the piles of rubble you might see pieces of bodies, severed hands, a head smashed in by rock. And perhaps you'll see a small foot outside the plot, separated from its owner's leg. No, this isn't like the images of war or massacres we see in newspapers and films. These terrifying images from our reality carve themselves onto our minds, living on even if the people in them are dead and gone. What we see can never be unseen. It's us, the ad-hoc rescue workers – the ones who dig through the rubble for survivors and the dead – who find ourselves within the frame of terror itself, and yet outside it at the same time, a forgotten piece of the tragedy.

The corpses still live on in my mind. Each time I pass by the hole that was once our neighbour Mohammed Naji's house, I stop to stare at the absurdity of war. Why did the Coalition missile target our neighbour's house? There is no convincing reason. Seems like it wasn't a mistake either, with all the rumours that had been flying around the neighbourhood for months: that the owner used to work as a cook for Ali Abdullah Saleh, or that the militia would meet here. But there wasn't a kernel of truth to any of it. The only people in the house were the father, his wife and their three children. I remember dawn that day when the roar of the fighter plane woke me. Like the rest of the Wadi al-Madam, I lived with the daily fear of being murdered. Militia shells began to fall on the neighbourhood. From one day to the next we paid our final respects to our dead. That dawn, in our neighbourhood, the fighter plane entered into the scene of war. It was very close to my house. When my walls shook and dust started to pour in through the window, I told myself it was madness for the Coalition to bomb our neighbourhood. The houses here are old and stuck to one another; they'd easily collapse on our heads. Surely they were bombing somewhere else, it just sounded close.

I went out at dawn and found the men of the neighbourhood, young and old, gathered in front of the crater the missile had made. They stared in disbelief. There wasn't a house there any more; our neighbour Mohammed Naji's home was gone. I saw fear in my neighbours' eyes, not sadness. Sadness is only for the victims' families, not the rescue workers or the bystanders. The rescue workers do what they can while the spectators think of the loss and bad luck that can befall anyone. Their sense of duty towards their neighbours unites them, while sadness is only for the victims' families. But there was no one from the victims' family with us; they were all lying under the rubble. No sound could be heard from the bottomless abyss.

It was pitch dark; there hasn't been any electricity in town since the start of the war. We had to sort ourselves out. There wasn't any Civil Defence or members of the resistance, just us, the neighbourhood residents. Getting our bearings in the dark was difficult, unable to see where we were stepping, let alone our hands or faces. Some people came with torches. I didn't have one, so I used my phone light to make my way. Our many shadows dug under the rubble, lifting the rocks together. The call for the dawn prayer rang out from the nearby mosque while our shadows raced to find someone alive. Sweat poured from our foreheads while we lost hope of finding survivors. Snatches of prayer drifted in from the mosque while we dug. Then we heard a feeble voice come from the hole. We started digging faster. Dirt covered Mohammed Naji's face. He was struggling to breathe, moaning and sobbing. He asked us, 'My children?' We told him his children were at their grandmother's. Some young men carried him away and took him to the hospital.

Finding the father alive gave us great hope, and we kept on digging in all directions around Mohammed's house. More rescue workers flocked to the scene, as well as photographers. I heard them shouting around me. I was seething. What did these idiots want? What were they taking photos of? There was no house, no people were left. But I let them be. Then, we started to pull out bodies. Pieces of them. You couldn't tell child from adult. When the morning light flooded us, we were still digging. And when we were certain there was no point in searching any further, we began to collect the bodies to bury them in the cemetery. Two days later, Mohammed, the father, died from the grief of losing his wife and children. A week later we found a child's foot in a back alley. We buried it in the cemetery as well.

When I pass by the hole, I stand there for a long time thinking of the war and its victims. Maybe we are all victims of this war started by the militia and the Coalition. All of them are killing us. But the spirits of those they kill still stand guard over the remains of their homes.

Adnan Saeed Amir

At dawn on Sunday, 1 November 2015, the Arab Coalition planes targeted Mohammed Naji Mohammed al-Shuja's home in the Wadi al-Madam neighbourhood of Taiz. His wife, Haniya Abdo Sharf al-Salwi (30 years old), was killed. His children, Asma Mohammed Naji Mohammed al-Shuja (12 years old), Amro Mohammed Naji Mohammed al-Shuja (6 years old), and Ibrahim Mohammed Naji Mohammed al-Shuja (one and a half years old) were all killed. Mohammed Naji Mohammed al-Shuja (35 years old), died on 7 November 2015 as a result of his wounds. Adnan Saeed Amir was one of the first rescue workers at the scene.

MY GIRLS, IF ONLY

You were all only a step from the front door. My girls, you'd be here safe with me right now, and I'd be so happy. You left the house cheerful, healthy, and came back on stretchers. Death came and plucked you like desert flowers. [*Atika Amin, an old woman in her sixties, cries. In the faint light of the small dark room, she sits curled up with her daughter Amani. Amani says, 'Your visit has made my mother sad all over again. We thought she was getting better.' The old woman's eyes cloud over and her voice grows hoarse; she no longer sees us before her. All she sees is the distance she walks from her front door to the Bab Musa riverbed.*]

The seventeenth night of Ramadan, a quarter to twelve. I remember how noisy the neighbourhood was, I remember the hustle and bustle, how loudly the children were playing, and the travelling voices of those praying in nearby mosques, giving me peace. I heard the drone of shelling, but it was far from my home. I prayed and lay on my bed, waiting for my daughters to return from the nearby mosque. I was still awake when my daughter Ishraq returned with her niece Muna. They had met in the mosque and agreed with my other daughter, Samar, to meet up in the souk later. My granddaughter Khawla was watching a show on television, and I convinced her to go along. If I had known what was going to happen, I would have stopped all of them from going out, but no one knows what fate has in store. I went back to lie down. Then, I heard my son yelling. My heart dropped and I ran to him. My eldest daughter Afrah was asking about why her daughter Muna was late, and before she could finish her question, the door opened, and two of my daughters and my granddaughter Muna were carried in on stretchers. Here, in front of me, in the courtyard, lay

151

the bodies of my daughters and granddaughter. I couldn't hear my own voice, my other girls crying, or my son's wife weeping. Grief has ravaged me, but what can I do? I say Alhamdulillah. Right? It is God's will, my girl. [*She cries and talks to herself.*]

My other granddaughter, Khawla, was between life and death; they told me she would improve. One of the neighbourhood children saw her after the shell fell. She was wounded, but still alive. They took her to the hospital. Khawla cried, her agony piercing right through me. She screamed, 'I don't want to die!' The shrapnel had gone into her heart, and her leg was ripped from her body. We took her to every possible hospital. She asked about her father, then her aunts. I told her, 'They're fine. What matters is that you get some rest darling.' But the doctors couldn't save her – none of them specialized in vascular surgery. My granddaughter bled out and was dead by dawn.

My heart is completely consumed by grief: I lived to see two of my daughters and granddaughters murdered, and escorted them to the grave. You can't even begin to comprehend such a catastrophe. Before it all, I used to worry about my son fighting for the government at the Sa'dah front. At the start of Ramadan he was wounded by a sniper's bullet, which made me lose sleep. Then my daughters and granddaughters were killed in the middle of Ramadan. I cry over them all the time; they still had so much life ahead of them. I'm overwhelmed with the grief of losing my granddaughter Khawla, my son's daughter. I had helped raise her since she was two months old. I see her everywhere. [*She cries and her daughter Amani comforts her.*]

My daughter Samar, my youngest, was married off at an early age. She now has three children – two girls and a boy. She'd always say, 'I don't want to die before Hammudi grows up.' I'd tell her, 'Don't worry about death my girl.' She'd respond, 'Umma, you don't know anything about being on the run from death, going from house to house. I learnt the meaning of fear from the air raids.' Three shells had hit her house. To save herself and her children, she moved from one house to the next. But a shell ended up killing her in the street. [*She cries.*] My heart breaks for you, Samar. Where are you and your children now? My grandchildren are scattered. They're with their other grandmother in Ibb; I don't know when I'll see them. [*'They're safe there and doing well,' her daughter reassures her. She nods wordlessly.*]

My granddaughter Muna is my daughter's firstborn, the apple of her eye. After her death, my daughter fled the city. She said, 'I can't live without Muna.' My other daughter, Ishraq, didn't go out much, but she was killed out in the street. She was hoping to be employed, but none of that matters beyond the grave. [*She cries.*] Fate, right? Perhaps I should say Alhamdulillah? Or? [*She asks herself and responds.*] We praise God in all things. But death snatched them suddenly, they still had so much to live for. I think of them constantly. How they were laughing that night, in such good spirits when leaving the house. They said, 'This Ramadan will be different, this year's will be better than ever before. The war is over and Eid will be better.' They went out laughing, full of life, and came back as corpses on stretchers.

Here in the courtyard, I saw them with my own eyes, one last time. I'll never forget them. Whenever I pass by in front of the dried-up riverbed, my chest tightens. I say, 'If only you had been quicker my girls, you would have reached home before the shell. If only you... [*she cries bitterly*] had been a bit quicker.'

Atika Amin

At midnight on Wednesday, 22 June 2016, the Houthi-Saleh militia bombed the Wadi al-Madam neighbourhood in Taiz. Her two daughters, Ishraq Mohammed Ali al-Shaybani (35 years old) and Samar Mohammed Ali al-Shaybani (31 years old), were killed, as well as her granddaughters, Muna Mohammed Othman (24 years old) and Khawla Mukhtar Mohammed Ali al-Shaybani (10 years old), and their neighbour Fahd Mohammed Qasim (40 years old).

I WAITED BUT SHE DIDN'T COME

My daughter doesn't ring the bell like that. Widad light-ly presses with her slender fingers as if playing a melody. Hearing it, my heart would skip and I'd run to open the door. Sometimes Widad would instead knock on the door in a special way, making a kind of music no one else could. I would know then that my daughter was behind the door. Widad always came to see me on her days off and on her way home from work. Even if I was tired from the day, or busy in the bedrooms, I'd drop everything and run to the door. Sometimes Widad would continue with her pranks, covering the peephole so I couldn't see through. I'd laugh with her and take part in her childish games. She'd sometimes change her voice. I'd say, 'Who's there?' And she'd say, 'I've come to take you away. Open up, Fattum!' I'd laugh wholeheartedly and say that this girl wasn't like her sisters. Widad would never grow up – she'd always be my little baby. I'd open the door and she'd fly into my arms. Light and life would follow her into our home. Now there's no one at the door, no sound comes from it, no knock, no bell, nothing. Only my own ghosts and a doorbell ringing in my ear. I return from my thoughts and realize Widad is no longer here. [*She falls silent and looks around.*]

Just a few months earlier, Widad had got married. I still remember her wedding day: it was January, a refreshing chill in the air, and the house was bursting with rela-tives and neighbours. I asked myself, when did this girl become a bride? I couldn't believe how time had flown, with my daughter leaving me for her husband's home. In the evening, Widad sat on the Kusha, and women danced around her on that bridal platform, their ulula-tions growing louder while I took in my darling daughter in her white dress. Then she was in the wedding car that would take her to her husband's home. In Sanaa, tradition dictates that the bride's mother doesn't ride with her. She says farewell in the wedding hall. But I don't care about traditions. This was Widad, the joy of my heart, and I personally escorted her to her husband's house. I sat next to her in the car, while she clapped and celebrated herself as a bride. Seeing her so happy, I forgot about how sad I was to lose her. I convinced myself, that's life. In a blink of an eye, your children are grown and living their own lives. I swung between wallowing in the void that Widad's absence left behind, and attempting to take my friends' advice to not be so tied up in my children's lives. But I still scheduled my life around Widad and her husband's visits to our home. It was always, 'Widad will come now – Widad, let's go out together – Widad, come have lunch with us today – Why don't you both come sleep at ours tonight? – When will you come back, Widad?' [*She falls silent.*]

I remember the last time she came over. It was after work, she and her husband; the three of us ate in the kitchen. On my right sat Ahmad, and Widad on my left. I looked carefully at Widad's face – it was the last time I saw them both happy. Widad was bursting with life, as if taking everything in one last time. I remember how they looked at and teased one another. Widad said, 'Mama, tomorrow's Thursday, my day off. I'll bake some biscuits for us so we'll both have them on Eid.' I told her, 'I'll come help you.' She said, 'No, Mama, don't worry yourself.' I didn't sense anything then, when saying goodbye to her, I thought that I'd see her the next day. Widad went down the stairs, laughing as she always did. But that day, she paused and looked at me, smiling. I told her, 'You'll fall! Look where you're going.' But she just stood there, smiling at me, waving at me, until she left.

The next day, I called her, but she didn't pick up. I told myself, 'Today's her day off, she must be resting.' I don't know how that day passed by: it felt like the longest day of my life. I was exhausted, a heaviness in my chest. I told myself maybe this tightness has something to do with the general atmosphere and my fear of what was to come, given it was the day of the festivities.[58] I didn't know how to pass the time. The whole day weighed down on me.

At half past three in the morning, I heard the first rocket explode – I ran out of my room. Our apartment lit up and the windows rattled as if we had been hit. 'Where's Widad?' I shouted. 'Where's Ahmad?' I couldn't breathe, I was suffocating. I told myself, they'll come now. Day or night, they always came over when the Coalition planes bombed Mount Attan. Widad and Ahmad would come to our house after dropping their neighbour off. Their home was close to ours, just ten minutes away. They had just moved there a few months ago. I wasn't comfortable with them living in Attan, I told them it was much too dangerous. Widad would respond, 'It's just temporary. Look: our furniture is packed up, even our bedroom. In a few days we'll move somewhere else.' But that dawn they were late. My sons and husband tried to calm me down. Then my sister informed me that Widad had told her that she and her husband were getting ready to leave. They'd pass by their neighbours Maha al-Samiie and her husband, and drop them both with relatives on the way over.

I stared out the window. Cars passed by. I kept saying, 'Widad and Ahmad will knock on the door any minute now. Or maybe they've just dropped off their neighbours.

58   On Thursday, 24 August 2017, the supporters of the People's Congress Party celebrated its founding anniversary in the al-Sabain square.

Maybe they're in that car coming over here now.' In that time, I tried to tune out any images of war I'd seen: the mangled corpses, tormented mothers, children being pulled out from under rubble. Time passed slowly while I kept a close eye on the roads. Neighbours and relatives set out to search the area, saying maybe they'd find them in a nearby alley. Maybe they were stuck in traffic. Or maybe they'd decided to go to Ahmad's family's home instead. But then came another explosion, the second rocket at Mount Attan. I became frantic. My son called Widad. She confirmed that she was now with their neighbour. The third rocket hit. I felt my heart racing. Widad's voice disappeared. My son heard glass being crushed, things falling. He heard her repeat, 'Oh God!', and then she was gone. My son called her husband's phone, but his voice was far away. He moaned but didn't respond to any questions.

Outside, it was dark everywhere. I strained to hear Widad and Ahmad's steps coming towards me. But there were only ambulance sirens. Whenever I heard one, I said that Widad must be in an ambulance. They both were fine, probably a few bruises at most. My son called from the Attan mountain pass saying, 'Mama, Widad's house is gone.' At that moment, I felt my spirit leave my body. But I still couldn't think of either of them as seriously harmed. The neighbourhood women reassured me that their husbands had gone there, and that Widad was fine. 'They pulled her out of the rubble, and she's now in hospital. You've got to go see her.' I started to gather together what Widad would need: a towel, clothes, soap. I asked them, 'What should I make her? She must be hungry.' They answered, 'She won't eat. Just go check on her.' It never occurred to me that they already knew Widad was dead.

Then I stood before the remains of my daughter's home; it had disappeared completely, no sign of life. The Coalition rocket had hit the neighbourhood elder's home, but the building that Widad used to live in had turned into a pile of rock and dirt. I would stare at those remains and think of her, thinking about how all these stones had been on top of her. How they must have crushed her. How she must have suffocated. I cried, not comprehending what had happened. I thought of every mother, every sister, every wife, every daughter who had lost a loved one in this war. That pain that seizes your heart, the pain that makes you stare aimlessly ahead at this pointless life. [*She falls silent.*]

At noon, they brought Widad to my home, dead. I had yet to fully wrap my head around her getting married and leaving my house, and now here she was before me, dead. I kept looking at her face, and thought of how her brothers couldn't identify her at first. I can pick my daughter out from a million people: the beauty spot on her face, her eyes, her eyebrows, her eyelids, the shape of her face, her fingers. Sure, her features may have changed, but I'd never mistake her; the light of my life that had been extinguished. Days before I had dreamed of Widad. I was stretched out on my bed staring at the ceiling when I saw Widad running and smiling, like she had on the stairs. That's the image I have of her drawn on the ceiling, laughing.

Yesterday, I passed by what had been Widad's home. Their belongings had been stolen. As I was searching for her wedding photo album, I saw the neighbourhood elder. I had heard from the neighbourhood women that he had escaped his own home just thirty minutes before the bombing. I couldn't control myself then. With all the grief and despair I felt inside, I yelled at him, 'May God punish you, the Coalition, and the Houthis. Why didn't you tell the others to get out when you knew a plane was going to bomb them? What did my daughter and the other innocent people do to deserve this?' He solemnly swore that he had been fleeing his home since the beginning of the war. I told myself, 'What does it matter now that my daughter is dead?' I stood there, on the edges of what had been Widad's home. Her nest of happiness. I looked at the home that had been destroyed: the remains, cartons just as they had been. A part of the bed was still in the bag. Pieces of the burnt carpet and curtains. I searched for her wedding album, but didn't find it. [*She falls silent while three of Widad's friends come in and offer their condolences.*]

All I have left of Widad is a small bag with the clothes she wore the last day she was alive: trousers, a t-shirt, her hair tie soaked in blood. Whenever I'm missing her, I wash the hair tie as best I can, and wring it out. I look at the blood run down the drain and think of the blood that has been spilled in this war, I think of my daughter Widad and all the other innocents who have been killed; I cry. I still was getting used to her having moved to her husband's home, and they took her from me. She was a bride, just beginning to celebrate her life.

I wash the blood now, the sad sound of a doorbell echoing in my ears. I know it's not Widad, they took her from me. [*She falls silent.*]

Fatima Ali Fadhil al-Misbahi

At 2.30 a.m. on Friday, 25 August 2017, the Arab Coalition planes fired four missiles at the home of Moassara Mohammed Moassar in the Attan mountain pass, Sanaa. In the first apartment that was hit, Faid Ahmad Muthanna (3 years), and Shuruq Ahmad Muthanna (8 years) were killed. In the second apartment, the father Basim Sadiq al-Sheikh and the mother Maha Abdel Wahab al-Samiee were also killed. The only survivor was their injured son, Sam Basim al-Sheikh (5 years). In the third apartment, a Palestinian citizen was killed, Mahmud al-Falastini (30 years old), and a Sudanese citizen, Wail Abdel Hafeez Farah (35 years). In the fourth apartment, Mohammed Mansour al-Reemi, his wife and children were all killed, and his brother-in-law Mohammed Saad as well. The only survivor was their daughter Bothayna Mohammed Mansour al-Reemi (6 years old). In the fifth apartment, Fatima Ali Fadhil al-Misbahi's daughter, Widad Abdallah Mahdi (20 years old), and her husband Ahmad Lutf al-Aseemi (30 years old) were killed, as well as ten other residents.

THEY DIDN'T DO A THING FOR MY SON

Your room is all white, Zayd, clean and tidy just like your room at home. Right above your bed we've put a small television. We thought you'd enjoy watching some matches and films once you wake up from your long slumber. On your right is a small white fridge, with different juices inside, and on top are some pots. Your mother's made your favourite foods, and she said, 'When Zayd wakes up, he'll want me to feed him.' In front of your bed is a smaller bed that I move around now and again. I lie down on it to watch over you every day. Sometimes your siblings come, and we watch you in shifts. We'll never leave you to the nurses. Just a week ago, Zayd, I had a stroke – I don't know what happened to me that day. The doctors said it was stress; my grief over you, my son, has eaten away at my health. When will you wake up? Your mother and siblings are missing you.

Every day I speak to Zayd, but there is no answer. Sometimes I realize I'm talking to myself and that Zayd is in another world, where perhaps my voice doesn't reach. In those moments I stare at his closed eyes, observing how he breathes under the oxygen mask, observing the tubes hooked up to his abdomen. Yellow urine, orange urine, white urine; Zayd, the dearest of my children, the war took you, my son, and broke my heart. [*He cries.*]

Ten months Zayd has been in a coma, clinically dead as the doctors say. I remember the last time he was awake, right after he was wounded. I cried bitterly that day. Zayd touched my fingers to reassure me he was okay. That was so many months ago, now there's no life in his body hooked up to all those devices; no sound comes from him, no movement. But I haven't lost hope. I tell myself, 'One day he'll wake from this coma, one day my son will come back as he was.' [*He cries.*]

When the war broke out in Taiz, we persevered for the first months in our house next to al-Noqta al-Rabea. But when our area turned into a war front, shells would fall on the neighbourhood all the time. Uphill from our house, the Republican Guard soldiers would gather, and downhill, elements of the resistance gathered in the riverbed. One day, the Republican Guard placed a cement barricade in front of our house. We didn't object, and just lived hidden away in the basement. But then a missile hit a shopping centre next to us; the fires extended to the buildings nearby. Our family scattered between Sanaa and al-Hawban, while my two sons Zayd and Raed stayed at home.

Zayd wasn't involved in the war that was taking the country by storm, nor was he part of the conflicts in the cities. He stayed away from politics. All my children were brought up like that. The warmongers in the neighbourhood were Zayd's friends, they were all local; they grew up with him and knew him very well. He shared the food supplies from our shop with them. He'd give half of it to the resistance and the other half to the Republican Guard. That's how Zayd was, he loved everyone. They all were his friends, no matter which party they belonged to, or which side of the war they stood on. But what good did it do him?

At ten on the seventh night of Ramadan, Zayd was on the roof filling up the water tanks. That's when a sniper from the resistance shot him. [*He cries.*] We rushed Zayd to the Yemen International Hospital; he was still conscious. After the operation, it seems that he regained full consciousness. On the second day he wrote to his uncle on a piece of paper, 'I want to see my face, take a picture of me.' His face had ballooned. I still have that piece of

163

paper. That day he asked about his mother and touched my fingers to reassure me. [*He falls silent.*]

That was the last thing he said before he slipped into the coma as a result of the doctors' and nurses' negligence. That day, the nurses had left him alone in his room. His hand was loose and when he coughed, he pulled out his oxygen tube. According to the hospital report, Zayd went for fifteen to twenty minutes without any oxygen. His heart started beating again, but he suffered substantial brain damage, and has been in a coma ever since. Tell me, who should we hold accountable? Who would you charge? The resistance sniper shot my son, who had done nothing to him, and the negligence of the hospital staff wiped out any hope of his recovery.

The bombing of the hospital started one morning. A shell damaged the outpatient clinic. They cut off the oxygen supply so that a fire wouldn't break out. Families were asked to take the patients with them. That morning I didn't know where we would take my son. Zayd needed oxygen to survive. We rented a minibus, an oxygen cylinder and headed for Sanaa. That's when our tragedy started in earnest. I remember how much land we crossed, eight hours of suffering, Zayd's body shaking while linked up to the oxygen. My heart ached with worry. We reached Sanaa at night, and took Zayd to the military hospital, but they refused to admit him, saying that they didn't have any free beds. We spoke with Ansar Allah,[59] and they said, 'Don't worry, we've made arrangements for Zayd at the Republic hospital.' We took Zayd straight there, and at the hospital gate they turned us away. We went to al-Thawra Hospital, and a nurse there told me to leave Zayd in the hallway. I told him, 'How can I leave him in the hallway? My son is in critical condition and needs oxygen!' [*He cries.*]

59 Translator note: the official name of the Houthi movement.

There was no one to help me save my son that night. At two in the morning, I admitted him to the police hospital. It was also overcrowded, but the gatekeeper took pity on me when I collapsed and started crying hysterically. I still remember howling that dawn, 'Where should I go? A stranger in my own country! Should I just let my son die? Never!' I knew that Zayd's condition had reached a point of no return when one of the doctors told me that he'd have to be treated in a specialist clinic abroad, to revive his spine and his brain. But I don't have the money to send him abroad. Even Yemen Airways[60] would make me pay the price of three seats for Zayd to go.

I'll never stop trying to save my son. I sold everything I have, and knocked on every door to save Zayd. I got in contact with Ansar Allah once more. I knew that they were just sending people away with empty excuses. They could easily find a way for Zayd to travel abroad and get him treated, like they did for their own wounded, but they didn't do a thing for my son. At first, the Houthis were interested in Zayd's case because the resistance in Taiz had shot him. But then they didn't end up doing anything for him. They said, 'Just take him from Aden airport to Cairo!' I told them that Zayd was in critical condition, and that he wouldn't last the exertion of a trip by land, not to mention how scared I was of crossing the al-Shuraijah checkpoint.[61] Besides, going down to Aden – it's no longer what it once was, the situation there has escalated, the people now blinded by hatred. They attacked our relatives down there, killing the father, mother, and son, saying that they were Afafesh, supporters of Ali

60   Yemen Airways didn't hesitate to double the suffering of
     citizens. It raised the price of one seat to a thousand dollars.
61   The checkpoint on the border between north and south Yemen
     before 1990.

Abdallah Saleh.

Hatred is everywhere though, I know that. Even in Taiz, the city where I've lived all my life, they stormed my house and burnt my shop down. They also set the house of a young man who worked in my shop on fire. All because they suspected my family supported Ali Abdullah Saleh. Yes, my father was the elder for the Jumhuri district, who spoke out against the youth revolution, but it still doesn't give them the right to storm my house and burn down my shop!

The war destroyed everything in this city, it changed the people and their morals. But all I care about now is saving my son. I'll do whatever it takes.

Ahmad Hassan al-Dhabibi

At midnight on Tuesday, 23 June 2015, a sniper from the resistance in Taiz shot Ahmad Hassan al-Dhabibi's son Zayd Ahmad Hassan al-Dhabibi (25 years old). Ahmad, the father, kept moving his son from one hospital to another during the year. I visited him in the Police Hospital. Despite his agony over his son and having sold everything for his treatment, he still had hope that Zayd would wake up some day from his coma. On 20 June 2016, I was informed of Zayd's death.

WHAT ARE SNIPERS MADE OF?

Whenever my father's eyes grow sad, it all comes back to me. That's when my patience runs out and I think of revenge. But snipers are disgusting, like rats, they're not like us at all. Nothing human about them; they kill for the thrill of it. They should carry their weapons out in the street, and take us out man to man – but they're too cowardly for that. Hiding there in the tallest building, taking pleasure in terrorizing us and knowing our entire lives now revolve around him. He retreats into darkness, taking aim with his rifle, and delights in killing his victims. I don't remember when the sniper appeared in our lives, like a phantom chasing our days and nights; while we were sleeping or when we had our backs turned to the war, unaware. We heard that the militia had stormed the al-Saudi building, the tallest building around here, which overlooks our whole neighbourhood. From then on, the sniper began to hunt lives day after day. What I remember well is how our daily lives shifted based on where the sniper was. He became a part of our lives, our fears, our nightmares.

The room in the al-Saudi building where the sniper had set himself up was right opposite our kitchen. We never saw him, but we heard the stories of his victims, and we'd see them sometimes lying in the alleyways or the main street. So we knew that the sniper was there, waiting for us to pass by him. He was waiting for us to slip up so he could murder us. Maybe he was smoking his cigarette absent-mindedly, bored with all our precautions, as we subconsciously anticipated his movements in the dark. Or maybe he was singing on cloud nine, laughing at our fear of death. The sniper turned the al-Saudi building into a tower of terror, one whose shadow grew among the people in our neighbourhood every day. Fear of the sniper limited our movements. Our homes were near the central prison in the Omran district, where the resistance had positioned themselves in farms, and the militia in al-Saleh park. Our home was in the middle, but we refused to desert it, afraid that the militia would rob our house, as they had done to others in our neighbourhood.

A year of war, and we had got used to protecting ourselves from the 'Saudi' sniper all the time. We locked up the kitchen and sat in our home, watching more people fall victim to him. We moved around like ghosts in our own home, fenced in by possible death from the window. We set up a makeshift kitchen in the hall, enough for our daily needs. The children were strictly forbidden from entering the kitchen. But all these precautions to avoid the sniper were useless when he shot my little brother.

Just thinking about that day, anger wells up inside me. We still hadn't come to terms with our mother's death. The sadness that dripped from my father's eyes kept us silent most of the time. I tried to lighten his mood and that of my younger siblings as much as I could. Worried, we would always keep an eye on the little ones so that they wouldn't go towards the kitchen. I don't know how my brother Nasser slipped out with Shaima that day, catching us off guard and making their way to the kitchen. Nasser must have wanted to pour whatever cold water was left into a thermos that was in the kitchen. All I recall is my father dashing off when Nasser screamed, 'Ya'ba!'

I'll never forget how my brother was lying in my father's arms, the kitchen window in the background taped shut with cardboard. I thought of how the sniper sidestepped all our ridiculous precautions. How pleased he must have been when he shot my brother. Revenge is a dark emotion, it eats into your heart and destroys you;

you can never get it out of your head.

If only they were waging war out in the streets, then I wouldn't feel this kind of hatred towards them. But for them to shoot a child in his own home – that is enough for me to grab a gun myself. When you see their arrogance, how they've closed off the city and killed civilians in their homes, you can't help but hate them with every bone in your body. When my mother fell ill, we couldn't take her to the hospital because al-Dehi was sealed off. We carried her on our backs, and when we couldn't find doctors in the city, we were forced to travel to Sanaa. This miserable life under the blockade, the humiliation, the insult of it all, has made me lose my mind.

Sometimes I get tired of my revenge fantasies: carrying a weapon and killing my brother's murderer a thousand times. But it doesn't relieve my rage. Even after people in our neighbourhood killed the al-Saudi building sniper and dragged him in the street, it was the same – the hate didn't leave my heart. His death won't bring back my brother and there are many more who'll just keep on targeting civilians.

My old father sighs deeply, and I know he's thinking of Nasser. Seeing how broken he is in his old age wounds me. Revenge is all I can think about. I know no good comes of such destructive feelings, but I feel so helpless, so enraged.

Sakhr Abdeljabbar Mohammed

On Saturday, 28 May 2016, a Houthi-Saleh militia sniper shot Sakhr's younger brother, Nasser Abdeljabbar Mohammed (10 years old), next to the central prison in Taiz. His sister, Shaima Abdeljabbar Mohammed (11 years old), was injured.

WHAT GOOD IS PATIENCE?

Sometimes I think that the murder of my brother and his family is just a figment of my imagination – at some point, overwhelmed by massacres, you start inventing tragedies – and that I'll find Munir banging on my door as usual to have lunch together. But my brother never comes, and he never bangs on my door. I turn away from the photos of Munir hanging on the wall, and return from my deep thoughts to reality, where neither my brother nor his family exist any longer. Only my family and I are stuck replaying their murder scene for eternity. Since their death, we numb our days with patience; but what good is patience when reality says you'll never see your brother or his family again? You have to get on with life – but I can't. When I remember Munir, my grief over him and his family eats me up. I think of how he might have been in those final moments; what did he say? Did he hold his children tightly like he used to, to make them feel safe? Was he thinking of the film he would produce if he survived this horror? Did Rami suffer? Did little Nouran think that this was some sort of game that a sick person threw her into, and that she'd just wake up tomorrow and go to nursery?

In war, the sound of a plane isn't just a plane. Each time, deep inside, you feel a disaster coming. At night we can't sleep, constantly on alert, our worries consuming us. We wonder about our loved ones: where are they now? What are they doing? Are they far enough from the bombing? Only once we make sure they're okay, can we then try to fall asleep. But while making enquiries about our loved ones, we never actually consider something could have happened to them, that the war is capable of taking them. When they don't answer our calls, we push such ideas out of our minds. Our eyes remain glued to the phone that just rings and rings and rings.

Munir didn't answer my calls. My eyes were stuck on the phone. It vibrated. I held my breath. It wasn't my brother, but a friend instead confirming my bad feeling: the Coalition planes had bombed the Beit Ma'yaad neighbourhood. Worry, panic, and my brother not picking up his phone, all of these drove me to step out that dawn and check on him. I still remember it all: the dark Sanaa streets, the faint glow of lights in the distance. I was drowning in dark thoughts. I tuned them out and clung on to some sort of hope, but when I reached Beit Ma'yaad, where my brother's home should have been, it was no longer there... [He falls silent.]

I stood at the remains of the building where my brother and his small family once lived. I searched for them in the dark, hoping someone had saved them. But there weren't any rescue workers, no police cars, or Civil Defence. Just a makeshift search party carelessly looking for limbs. At ten the next morning, they found my brother's family's limbs: his children Rami, Majed and Nouran, as well as his wife Suad. A catheter was still in Rami's hand, as he had been ill. My brother remained under the rubble, and they didn't recover him till a week later, after they knocked down what was left of the building.

There are no barracks or military camps next to my brother's home. People say they wanted to hit the al-Ghanami warehouse. Liars. Murderers. The hangar was used as a warehouse for cooking oils, and there was no reason to bomb it. I hold the Arab Coalition responsible for killing my brother and his family. They were defenceless. Civilians. Innocent. We haven't been granted the right to know why they were murdered, and what they had done to deserve this.

Nothing and no one can compensate me for losing my brother, nothing. They can never bring him or his family back. But I trust that God sees everything and that God will avenge us.

Fawaz Muqbil al-Hakimi

At 9 p.m. on Tuesday, 9 February 2016, Arab Coalition planes bombed the home of his brother, Munir Muqbil al-Hakimi (40 years old), a producer in Yemeni television, in the Beit Ma'yaad neighbourhood in Sanaa. Munir, his wife Suad Hajira (34 years old), also a producer in Yemeni television, and their three children, Rami Munir Muqbil al-Hakimi (12 years old), Majed Munir Muqbil al-Hakimi (10 years old), and Nouran Munir al-Hakimi (5 years old) were all killed.

THE PIGEONS NO LONGER COME BY

Pigeons always remind me of my brother. Whenever I hear cooing, my brother Amjad appears before me. I open the window and try to coax it into my room; I put seeds on the window sill and move away, but the pigeon still doesn't come. It hovers a little way from the window. Pigeons don't like me, but they loved Amjad.

Amjad's obsession with pigeons started long ago, and it grew as he did. My brothers and I used to tease him for it, but that didn't bother Amjad. His passion for pigeons was only matched by his zest for life. I don't remember exactly when Amjad's relationship with pigeons started, when he bought or touched his first one. His childhood bond with them grew stronger as he raised them. From their cooing, we'd grow aware of more and more pigeons on the roof. Sometimes we'd catch Amjad holding one while he sang to it. Come to think of it, it wasn't Amjad who found the pigeons, but it was they who came to him – in the dozens, from different cities and countries, all in search of him.

For many years, we would hear the flutter of wings from the roof of our house all day long. When their flapping grew faster, we knew that Amjad was up there for his usual visit: feeding them, cleaning them, treating them for any ailments, and singing to them. Sometimes we'd forget that Amjad was up there. We'd get bored of his pigeon stories. We were always fascinated, however, by how he fed them: he'd chew the food up in this mouth and then handfeed the baby pigeons. If a pigeon fell ill, he nursed it back to health. Only when everything was done, would he come back down to chat with us.

With no pigeons now in the shadow of the house, I feel Amjad's absence. I remember how, a week before it all went wrong, Amjad and my other brother Mohammed were so pleased to have got a job at a clothes shop nearby. After the war destroyed my father's business and he couldn't find work, Amjad had become the sole breadwinner for the family. My father was so happy that Amjad and Mohammed had found work. Eid was right around the corner, and even with the war on, we were busy with preparations. My mother went out to buy new clothes for my siblings, while I stayed home with the little ones. We waited for my mother to come back with the rest of our family. I still remember the boom of the shells at sunset that day. That's when we heard a boy's scream.

Amjad was killed and Mohammed's spine was seriously injured. Mohammed is now paralysed and lies in bed all the time, unable to move. My heart aches to look at him. My mother and father sold everything they had to pay for his treatment. They moved from city to city to save Mohammed from complete paralysis.

We're now alone – my younger siblings and I collected in this room. We endure our grief over our family's disaster. Sometimes my grandmother comes to stay with us in the house so that we don't feel afraid, all alone. My parents left for Aden a month ago, in a desperate attempt to get Mohammed medical treatment. I think of what happened to our home, of the war that killed us the day it killed our brother Amjad. I think of the pigeons that no longer come by.

Mihyal Jamal Saleh

At 5.30 p.m. on Saturday, 19 September 2015, Houthi-Saleh militia bombed the Farah Mall in the Masbah al-A'la in Taiz. Mihyal's brother Amjad Jamal Saleh (17 years old) was killed along with three others. Another brother of Mihyal's,

Mohammed Jamal Saleh (15 years old), was seriously injured.

RUNNING ON THE DAY OF NUQUM

It was a day that no one will forget in the history of Sinan neighbourhood, let alone the history of the war. A day we mourn the loss of our family and friends. My siblings and I remember that day well, when the Coalition planes bombed Jabal Nuqum. We hadn't heard the usual shelling of the mountain while we were at home. Our windows would shake and the doors fling wide open, then slam shut. We would hide under the beds or in the corners of the room until the shelling subsided. But that day was different. We saw the instruments of death that flew around the mountain right before our eyes; we saw it face to face, as if seeing the war for the very first time.

We were on our way back from my sister's house. Whenever there was shelling, we'd never stay in our house by Jabal Nuqum, and flee to my sister's home instead, staying there until we were sure the planes wouldn't come back to bomb the mountain. So that afternoon, we'd been convinced it was finally safe to go outside, not considering that war follows its own rules. After the air strike, the first missile from the weapons storehouse on Jabal Nuqum exploded. We were close to death at the Nasr roundabout; I saw the shine of the missile and its shrapnel cutting through the air. My heart raced, my throat dried up. Looking around, I was panicked by what I saw. Neighbours and passers-by were running, pushing one another, screaming, stammering cut-off words, incomprehensible. And when the missiles flew into the air in all directions from the mountain – I ran, too.

That's right, I ran. I remember running amidst a human flood, all crammed in at the foot of the mountain: men carrying children on their shoulders, teenagers running barefoot, women running cradling their little ones, children overtaking adults. And me, I was running: my hands, my feet, my eyes, everything in me was running. I couldn't breathe, but I kept running. My mother ran next to me, my sisters Yasmin and Ghadeer ran. We dragged my sister's children behind us and didn't turn round despite their crying.

Nowhere to hide from the flying missile pieces. We just ran straight ahead with everyone else, following them at every turn. Shrapnel fell around us and killed some. In front of us was a man who was hit in the head – he collapsed, blood pooling around him. We kept on running and didn't turn round. Shops were closed. There wasn't even a hole for us to crawl into to escape death. While running, we saw an open communications centre. My mother, sisters, I, and others dashed inside to seek shelter. But the employee threw us out, so we kept running.

With great difficulty, a heavily pregnant woman ran with us. Her husband pulled her along. She forced herself forward while blood ran down her legs. We ran with everything we had. Sometimes we'd stop when we heard the sound of some shrapnel nearby, allowing it to whizz past. My elder sister took off her shoes and ran barefoot. She stepped on some broken glass in the street, and her feet were bleeding, but she kept on running. My father couldn't run like us, he suffered from diabetes and high blood pressure. I remember him sitting in front of our house, his panicked eyes following his children and the neighbours running for their lives. We couldn't stop to pull him along. When I looked at him, my grief made it difficult to breathe. My younger sister Yasmin dragged her nephew along with great difficulty. When she couldn't manage any more, she hid with him under a broken-down car. With her arms wrapped tightly around Abudi, I watched her tremble. An old man reassured her,

'Don't worry my girl. You're safe now. Don't worry.' Just as he finished his words, a piece of shrapnel split his head in two, and he dropped dead next to my sister.

After we left Nasr roundabout behind, some kind-hearted families opened up the basement of one of the buildings, and we hid out there with some neighbours. I saw one of my neighbours who had just given birth only a few days before. She lay curled up with her newborn and their belongings.

We remained there, silent. Listening to the footsteps of those still running past, and shrapnel whistling as it hit the ground. When silence finally fell, ambulances began to rush to our neighbourhood. It was eight o'clock at night.

We'll remember that day for the rest of our lives. When we are old, we'll tell our children about it. They won't know the meaning of running on the day of Nuqum. A day where dozens of our neighbours were killed: men, women and children. Two of them were my brother Abdelrahman's friends, and one of my sister's friends was injured by the shrapnel – she can't walk to this day. My sister Yasmin still lives with the nightmare of the man whose head split in two.

Raqiyya Faraj

At 4.30 p.m. on 21 May 2015, Arab Coalition planes bombed Jabal Nuqum in Sanaa, exploding an arsenal above the people below. Twenty civilians were killed.

THEY WILL NEVER GET ENOUGH
OF OUR BLOOD

Stuck in his ways, as old people often are, my husband liked to sleep in the courtyard of our house on hot days. Looking up at the sky soothed his anxious spirit. I don't know what thoughts he had while sleeping there, what calming dreams the sky gave him. But my spirit never settles, fear lives in my heart, and I'm never sure if the sun will rise tomorrow or if a shell will kill us instead.

This has been our life since the beginning of the war. We, the residents of al-Zahra neighbourhood,[62] live in constant fear of every shell fired from the cannon's mouth, every scratch at our shut doors, every clack of reloading ammunition, every victory whistle, sung by fighters when their shells hit the enemy. Fear makes itself at home in our hearts and never leaves. We, whose neighbourhood has been made into a warzone, opening us to impending death from the hill where the Sofitel is, and the Special Security Forces camp where the militia and the Republican Guard forces are stationed. Shells fall all the time, day and night, down from the hill towards our neighbourhood. And then the young men of the resistance in our neighbourhood shoot back. Sometimes a man of tender age from the resistance would be killed, and the heartbreak their mothers suffered would seize me as well. Sometimes innocent civilians from our neighbourhood would die too. Our eyes would grow puffy from all the crying.

We organize our days around the unrelenting shelling. During the day, we time our housework around when the shells strike, and at night we know that the fighters

62 Located on the east of Taiz, overlooking the hills that are
    controlled by the militia, it is one of the areas worst affected
    by the war.

get their thrills from terrorizing us. Not a single one of us still here dares to light a candle – the snipers might see us. After we've made sure to draw the curtains and close off the windows with cardboard, we walk around with small torches fastened atop our heads or carrying lanterns, making sure no light gets outside to the snipers. We're like cavemen; always in the dark. During the day we don't go out unless absolutely necessary because the boom of the shelling and zinging of bullets is non-stop. Sometimes, when we can't find anything to eat, we risk crossing the street and going to the nearest shop. But when we can't find what we need there, we just come back hungry. No one comes to our neighbourhood, no aid organizations, no journalists – they all fear the shells and snipers' bullets. They no longer care what happens to us. When we were still able to go to other neighbourhoods, and we'd come across people from the city, they couldn't believe that we lived in al-Zahra neighbourhood. From a distance, city dwellers are horrified when they see our houses riddled with bullet holes and hit by shelling, or when they see a mosque minaret tumble down. They run away, never daring to climb up to our neighbourhood.

Months into the war, many of our neighbours fled, afraid of the shelling, but our family and the family next door stayed. At one point we decided to flee to our village in al-Aabus. When we arrived there, the Coalition planes started to bomb the village, and fearing for our lives, we moved back to our home here in al-Zahra. That day, my husband slept in the courtyard. I was terrified when a shell fell on our roof, tearing apart the upstairs. Dust filled my lungs. When I opened my eyes and saw my children, I thanked God. But then I remembered my husband who suffered from liver disease. We couldn't get him to a hospital. The missiles kept on falling on our neighbourhood, and the young men of the resistance responded to the militia's bombing. Our houses shook. My husband moaned in pain and we just kept quiet.

Helplessness is a destructive feeling. When you can't do a thing to save the life of someone you love, you consider risking going out in the middle of the war, and begging the fighters to give you some time to take your sick husband to the nearest hospital. But they'll never stop. My husband, the father of my children, languished day after day, and we couldn't do anything. I watched him die a slow death, soundlessly, never complaining. My husband died before my eyes and those of his children one night. We couldn't even give him a proper burial. They stopped us honouring him in his passing when they stopped us taking him to the hospital – they simply sped up his death. The shells rained on our neighbourhood more than ever before, and we stayed up late keeping watch over his corpse, thinking of ways to bury him. For days we stared at his body. I couldn't believe that he'd died and left us alone. [*She cries.*] We got in contact with relatives, but they couldn't help us. They lived too far away. After some days, finally one relative, with great difficulty, was able to get my husband's body out of the house and bury him in al-Hawban.

We don't want anything from this life. All we want is for this war to end. We'll persevere through the fear and famine, but we can't keep living with death day in, day out. When I went back to my home some months after my husband died, the war was still raging, paying no attention to any of our dreams, or all the horrors we had endured. I was going up the stairs when a missile fell on my neighbour's home. A piece of shrapnel injured their son, cutting through his neck. I fell to the ground, and the joint in my foot snapped out of place. I sobbed. Yes,

I sobbed at how this war will never get enough of our blood.

Hajja Nadheera Abdelwadud

The residents of al-Zahra neighbourhood of Taiz live under the most difficult of circumstances, as the neighbourhood is located at the frontline between the fighting parties. Most of the residents have fled except for those who couldn't because of their poor economic conditions. I met Hajja Nadheera Abdelwadud in the al-Zahra neighbourhood. The audio recording is interrupted by militia cannons and sniper bullets piercing the roof opposite. Hajja Nadheera, who now lives with her daughter in al-Zahra neighbourhood, wasn't able to bury her husband in a decent manner. He died without her being able to help him, and she hasn't been able to get a death certificate with his date of demise because they buried him secretly at night, only after getting his corpse out of the neighbourhood with great difficulty.

I HAVE NO ONE LEFT

Taha is sleeping, so I can finally rest a bit. I think of the house, empty of life now they're gone. The ruckus of my two nephews has faded into quiet. The chatter of my two other brothers has disappeared as well, leaving just me and my younger brother Taha in this darkness. I observe his breathing, look at his eyes staring off into the distance, not knowing what he's looking at or what he sees. I've grown up but Taha hasn't. He's a year younger than me, but time stopped for him; he doesn't grow like we do. The doctors diagnosed him with cerebral atrophy. Taha doesn't know what's happening around us, who died, who survived; he isn't affected by the ups and downs of life like we are. He has all the time in the world. Sometimes I envy his blissful ignorance.

After my mother's death about a year ago, Taha suffered an anxiety attack. He curled up into a ball and we couldn't get him to calm down. My brothers Ahmad and Mustafa would help me look after him, taking him out into the street to play. But taking care of Taha has become my sole duty in this life. I'm the only daughter in our family. I run after Taha from one place to another, making sure he doesn't get hurt. He's like a twenty-nine-year-old child. I force him to eat, rock him to sleep, and when he finally drifts off, my nightmares come alive.

The house is empty now without them. It's just me, Taha, and my brother's wife – her husband and their children were killed. Each of us sits in her own world, crying over the loss of our loved ones. I lost my two dear brothers, they were all the family I had left in this life. Sometimes I feel suffocated by this home and the memories that won't leave me alone. I want to get out and walk anywhere, far from here, but I can't. I'm a prisoner within these four walls. I remember the day it all came crashing down. My brother Ahmad had taken us to the seaside. The waves crashed into the rocks lining the shore, and seagulls circled above us. I don't remember what we talked about then; it's as if a screen is veiling everything from me. All I remember is the peace and familiarity that blanketed us. My brother's sons Ramzi and Ramez were laughing with Taha. He was more of a kid than them, taken in by the waves crashing, the seagulls, and the crows up above. There was no fear or sadness in me, other than the grief over my mother's passing – it still hadn't been a year. I was happy when I was with my brother's family, and didn't think that outing would be the last joyful moment of my life.

Sometimes when I sit alone, I see Mustafa within the last memory I have of him: he's come out of the bath, still dripping wet, and smiles at us. Half an hour later, the first rocket explodes. It was close to us but we didn't know exactly where the explosion took place. When Ahmad came to check on us, he told us that the Coalition forces had bombed the Presidential Palace. He added, 'I'm going to the funeral for our neighbour, Mohammed Abdo.' The children surrounded him and insisted they go along.

As she always did at that time of day, my sister-in-law was preparing lunch, while I got Taha's milk ready for him to drink with his medicine. First I heard a shrill whistle that almost burst my eardrums. Then the missile fell. It must be an earthquake, I thought. The walls shook and the wooden room divider fell to the ground. A thick cloud of dust filled the house, and we couldn't see anything. We heard screams outside. Taha jumped from his place and ran towards the door. I ran after him and grabbed him. It grew late, and finally our older brother came over and informed us that my other two brothers and nephews had been killed. [*She cries.*]

The plane was still circling overhead. Indistinct figures dug for corpses under the rubble of collapsed houses. The dust everywhere made it difficult to see anything except for the shadows of men moving with torches and their phone lights. I heard them as they counted the dead, survivors and injured. I broke down. My voice was imprisoned inside me. I cried and tried to pull myself together for Taha's sake, who was running from one end of the house to the next, alarmed by the sound of the strike. But he didn't know what had happened, and I didn't tell him that they had bombed the house where the funeral was happening; that his brothers and dozens of other mourners had been killed; that the houses in the neighbourhood had been destroyed and fallen on the heads of those inside.

Only when Taha calmed down did I take stock of what was around me: an ambulance at our front door. I saw the bodies of my brothers Mustafa and Ahmad, and Ahmad's sons Ramzi and Ramez. Ahmad's body had been split in two. They wouldn't let me see Mustafa's face, saying that it was too deformed. I said that I wanted to see his face whatever shape it was in. [*She cries and whimpers.*] They murdered my brother Mustafa, a handsome man in his thirties, soon to be married. Mustafa didn't have a face any more, there was nothing but blood around his head. When I lifted the blanket off his face, I saw that half of his head was missing; it was as if a knife had sliced through his forehead and hair, leaving the brain cavity empty. [*Her voice chokes and she cries.*] I look over at Taha who smiles at me naively. His silence and confusion are nearly the end of me. Taha doesn't know what has happened to us, he doesn't know that Mustafa, who used to take him everywhere, is dead.

I feel death in every corner of our house: in the walls, in the rooms, in the kitchen. I remember my brothers and my nephews, their chatter, their noisemaking, their aspirations. On the morning it happened, my nephew Ramez had been sitting in my lap. He said, 'I love you, Khala.' 'And I love you, Ramez,' I answered. 'Khala, I miss Gedda – when will we see her?' 'Why do you say that?' I asked him. 'Because I miss her, Khala,' he responded. 'She always gets her hookah ready and then tells me stories, and I miss Gedda's stories.'

Their grandma's stories aren't anything like the horror stories I'm living in now. I have nothing after my brothers' deaths. I can't cry in front of Taha, I'm afraid of him having another anxiety attack. Sometimes he asks me, 'Where's Ahmad? Where's Mustafa?' I tell him, 'Say, may they rest in peace.' But he doesn't understand what I say, he just looks up at the sky, and I think maybe he is saying rest in peace in his own way. I don't know who told Taha a few days after it all happened that his brothers and his nephews had been killed. He then asked me, 'Is Ahmad dead?' 'Yes, Taha.' 'Mustafa, dead?' 'Yes, Taha.' 'Ramzi, and Ramez, dead?' 'Yes, Taha. They've gone and left me alone, they've gone and left me alone.' I mourn my brothers and how alone I am. I try to calm Taha down, I can't take another anxiety attack.

I'm alone now. The Coalition planes have killed my brothers without shame. It's their fault that I can't see them any more, and live under their protection. I've stayed here like the walls of this empty house. No one turns to me and says, 'What's wrong Salwa?' Salwa is exhausted, Salwa swallows her fury so Taha won't get scared, because all Taha has left in this world is Salwa.

Salwa Ali Mohammado

186

At 9.00 a.m. on Thursday, 22 September 2016, Arab Coalition planes bombed a funeral service in the al-Hunud neighbourhood of al-Hudaydah. In addition to dozens of civilians, Salwa's brother Ahmad Ali Mohammado (40 years old), his sons Ramez Ahmad Ali Mohammado (8 years old) and Ramzi Ahmad Ali Mohammado (4 years old), and their brother Mustafa Ali Mohammado (30 years old) were all killed.

THE DOG DOESN'T BARK

I have no home any more. I've been living here in this shop since the war came to the city. I don't know how long ago we fled – I no longer feel the days go by or time passing. I don't remember the exact day we had to run from our home, but I remember how hot it was. The Asr call to prayer went out from the nearby mosque, punctuated by the whistling of shells the militia were dropping on the Ussaifira souk, where we lived. We tiptoed, scared stiff by the sniper shooting down passing pedestrians. We hated the idea of fleeing, but after a shell hit our home, we feared that our children would die next, and decided to leave. We packed our few clothes into a single suitcase and left everything else behind: our furniture and our entire small world.

We have no home now, living in a space no bigger than four square metres: me, my husband, and my three children along with my pregnant sister's family, her husband (who is also my husband's brother), and their two daughters. We can't move in this tiny space. We adults walk carefully, trying not to bump into each other, though the children have transformed the space into a small playground. Empty cardboard boxes divide up our overlapping worlds, imaginary borders between us so at night the children know their place. During the day, we're all round one table for breakfast, lunch and dinner. Me and my sister sit, anxious about making ends meet. We remember life before the war, when we had our own place, and our husbands would slog away washing car windows. Their wages were barely enough for us to scrape by, but we were safe. We weren't dependent on charity. Now my husband lives in a world of his own, speaking to ghosts.

A blue curtain separates us from what's happening

out on the street, and there's an iron door that we only close at night because of how hot it gets. There aren't any windows in the shop for a breeze to slip in, so we leave the iron door open most of the time. When the blue curtain twitches, we know there's a visitor for us. We practically live on the street: we hear the cars honking, passers-by yelling, and everything else that goes on in our neighbourhood. When a fight breaks out, we wait anxiously to see what will happen next. Our hearts grow tender at the shrieks of the starving madman. And when we tire of all the racket that drains our days and nights, we close our eyes in the darkness between the peeling walls. Our lives have been playing out within this tiny space since the war started. In the hot months, the air is so thick we can barely breathe, and we remember how long we've been away from home. The sound of children crying and adults bickering is like an unending choir. In the winter months our limbs freeze on the cold tiles, and our joints grow stiff on the worn-out, thinning mattresses.

We can forget our misery and fear of the future, we can forget that we need others to survive. But we can never forget our grief over Mohammed, our youngest son. When he stands quietly without moving, and a hesitant smile appears on his lips – that's when I think how bitter life is. When his careful hands grope the wall so he won't fall, that's when I want to die. When he plays with his cousins and falls on the ground, without grumbling; my agony suffocates me. When he stands in the doorway to the shop and hears the neighbourhood children yelling, sadness clear on his face – I die another time. When he forgets his misfortune, and makes his way out onto the street, and car horns shriek so that they won't run him over; he stands there frozen and I run to him sobbing. When he wakes up from his nightmares, soaked in sweat, and tells me about the dog that was staring at him, my patience runs out and I tell my husband about the nightmares. But my husband just babbles to himself in drawn-out delusions, and doesn't pay me any mind. I can't get him out of his shock, and I can't get him to a psychiatrist. I'm bound in all these shackles that pull at me from my head.

That afternoon, when my husband's shock began and he shut himself away in a world I know nothing about, we had been living in the shop for over a month. We didn't know that tragedy would follow us here. That day, I was behind the blue curtain you see here, and Mohammed was standing outside the iron door, watching the neighbourhood children get together. Just a few minutes later, I heard the sound of a shell explode. When I saw my husband cradling Mohammed in his arms, I thought he was dead. There were bodies everywhere in the street next to our shop. [*She falls silent.*]

The shrapnel pierced my son's body and shattered his feet, but the real tragedy was that Mohammed lost his sight. Some shrapnel entered his right eye, and doctors were unable to salvage his vision. His left eye was all he had left, but there were also some fragments stuck in it, and he could only see out of less than half of it. To save his left eye, we went to every single hospital, and they all said the same thing: we had to take him abroad as quickly as possible to save him from going completely blind.

Days grew into months while we were stuck, unable to even scrape together enough for us to eat, while each day Mohammed was getting closer and closer to total blindness. Sometimes he sits silent in the corner, while his cousins play around him. Images and other things swim around in his left eye, he can no longer tell what is what, he says. The long night is starting to fall. Mohammed tells me the shadow of the dog he's been seeing in his eye since the shelling has become clearer. The dog stares at him the whole time, but hasn't barked once. His injured body trembles. I rock him to get him to sleep, but he still tosses and turns in his dark world. In that same darkness, my husband's mumbling grows louder, talking to people only he can see.

I now live in this shop, the noise of the street around me. I wait for some kind soul who'll give us a meal so that we don't starve to death. But I never get angry, it's a war after all.

Nawal Sayf Abdo Tahir

Nawal Sayf Abdo Tahir lives with her husband, her children, her sister, her brother-in-law, and their children in a shop next to al-Hazmi grocery in the al-Masbah al-Asfal neighbourhood in Taiz. It is a small shop with no protection from the cold, completely unsuitable to live in. Nawal, her family, and her sister's family live off intermittent handouts. Her son Mohammed Muaz Ahmad Khaled (9 years old) was injured on Monday, 21 September 2015 by a shell that Houthi-Saleh militia dropped on some passers-by that were next to the shop in Taiz. Mohammed was injured in the eyes, and in danger of going blind. Her husband has been in a state of mental confusion since the event. I visited her in the shop where they live. Mohammed asked me, 'When will the war end Aunty? I want to play football outside.' Mohammed doesn't comprehend that he will never see again.

ONE OF THEM LET OUT AN 'AH'

Whenever I hear a shell explode or a plane roar, I tear open our front door and run in any direction out into the streets – I run and run, away from the evil that has snatched my family, the evil that chases me wherever I go. I run and don't want to stop, and in that moment I am free; my memories can't catch me. Sometimes a relative grabs me saying, 'Nothing's going to happen Ezzeya, everything will be fine.' But I just close my ears to their pleading, distancing myself like I always do when I want to protect myself from my memories, not to think of anything. With only the white sky blanketing me. No bodies. No screaming. No cries for help. No severed heads.

In these moments of peace, my children come alive again, and return to me. We are together again like old times. But evil returns with the bang of a gunshot, explosion of a shell, or roar of an airplane – that's when the memories come back. [*She falls silent and curls into herself.*]

At first, my husband wanted to help me forget the tragedy. We had to leave our home. I remember how I screamed that night once the tranquillizers wore off; I pushed them away as hard as I could. All I wanted was to go back home, to my children. I couldn't sleep, and just stared at the bodies of my children as they went round my head. We rented another house in al-Hawban. My husband said, 'You'll calm down here, and then they can perform the operation.' The hospital was near the house, but the sedatives were no good at silencing my memories. The noise of shelling and explosion of rockets froze me on the spot. My body would shudder with fever. I really felt sorry for my husband, exhausted by my illness and the loss of his children and first wife. We left al-Hawban for Sanaa to escape the noise of the shelling, and stayed there for ten months. I don't know how those days passed – I didn't feel time at all. I was in shock, not aware of what anyone was saying. I saw people around me, but I couldn't speak; I was still stuck in the moment it all happened.

The air raids jolted me out of my stupor, bringing fear back into my heart each time. I cried, trying to run from where I was. I wasn't getting any better, so my husband decided we should go back to our home in Taiz. He told me it was the best way to face and reconcile with my memories, to go back to the place it all happened, but I just couldn't come to terms with my loss. When I got home, the gates of my memory opened up to all the ghosts. Going back to my home was like reopening the wounds, bringing back all the details of what I went through with my children, my husband's first wife, and our neighbour. I remember how my husband's first wife had been that morning – wearing a new dress. My two daughters Rehab and Rabab were chatting away next to me. My son Hamza laughed, and then the next thing I know, he's dead on the ground. [*She sobs, and the women around her in the room encourage her, saying 'Stay strong, Ezzeya.' She smiles faintly, staring at the women, and then sighs. She starts talking once more.*]

War came to the city and brought the houses down on the heads of those inside, taking away their only source of shelter. We only realized what was happening when we saw the armed men on the street. I didn't think of death at that point, but when the shells hit al-Ashbat neighbourhood from the hills where the militia had stationed themselves, I got really scared. The explosion rocked our house to its foundations. We didn't know then where the shell had hit. The panic of the men terrified us more than anything; we heard them running through the neighbourhood. There were no casualties at first, but fear reigned in everyone's hearts. Many families fled the neighbourhood;

I remember women gathering in the street, their children surrounding them. I sensed their alarm while they waited anxiously for their husbands to return carrying the keys to their abandoned homes.

Only our house, and that of my brother-in-law and sister remained standing in the dust, in the face of war. It was out of the question for my husband to leave. 'We're a large family,' he said. 'Where do you want us to go?' My eldest daughter Rabab insisted we leave home like everyone else. Her pleading had started long before, after her father had made the decision to stay. She seethed, 'None of you will leave this house until someone is dead!' Oh my girl, if only we had listened to you. [*She weeps bitterly.*]

I felt heat deep inside as if I was on fire. I splashed my face and body with some water, but the heat continued to rise. I wanted to leave the house, stretch my legs a bit, and calm down. But I tossed the idea aside because it was better to stay here on the ground floor, where my entire family was gathered. It was a safe enough place, we thought. The windows on the ground floor did not overlook a space that might be hit by a shell. That's what we thought when we left the upstairs, after a shell had hit destroying our water tank and shattering our windows. On that morning, we prepared breakfast for the family. My girls cleaned the house. The other women of the family and neighbours were gathered in the room facing the street. The men were in the home of my husband's son, opposite ours. Suddenly, shells started to fall on the neighbourhood. The first hit the house next door. Some shrapnel flew inside our house. When it grew close to eleven o'clock, I went to prepare lunch. I didn't hear the second shell that hit our courtyard. The corner of the room was hit. Later, I was told that Mohammed, my husband's son from his first marriage, was the first to be wounded.

I choked on the smoke, unable to see around me. The dust went into my eyes and nose; a few minutes later, it settled. From one end of the living room to the other, there were bodies; nowhere for me to walk without stepping on corpses. The first one I recognized at the back of the living room was my son Hamza. The was a large hole in his head, and his brains were on the ground next to him. [*She cries.*] With my hands drenched in blood, I picked up the sticky pulp and tried to put it back into his skull cavity. A piece of shrapnel had pierced my body, but I didn't feel it. I was too absorbed in my desperate attempt to put the brains back in their rightful place. I knew that my son wouldn't live. My hands trembled at the thought, but I kept trying. I turned round and saw my husband's first wife lying out flat on the ground. Then I saw my two daughters, Rehab and Rabab, lifeless bodies. Then our neighbour Sabah and two of her daughters. No life in them at all, only Hiba, my neighbour's other daughter was still hanging on. I saw her exhaling, the air coming out from an opening in her back. My neighbour's eyes were on me. She muttered feeble words, but I couldn't understand what she was saying, like she was trying to ask something of me. I still remember her eyes full of fear, and her lips, trying to form words. [*She cries.*]

I don't know what I was seeing, was all this a nightmare or reality? Soaked in my son's blood, my face swollen, full of shrapnel. My husband came in. He didn't know that the shell had killed nearly everyone in the room. But then he saw them. His wife, then his daughters, and his son, and our neighbour's family. He embraced his wife and then ran out into the street. 'My children? This is too much!' [*Ezzeya cries, and a woman next to her seated in the middle of the room keeps saying, 'Thank God, Ezzeya.' She falls silent and looks at the woman stunned.*]

I'm there, in the middle of the bodies, everything in me is dead, except for my hands. Some sort of power comes to my hands while they try to put the brains back in my son's head. Then I heard an 'ah' come from the mouth of one of them, a sigh, a final exhalation after wrestling against intense pain. Was the 'ah' from one of my daughters' mouths? Or from my son? Or from my husband's wife? My neighbour? Her daughter? After that, everything went quiet. [*She cries.*]

I don't sleep; no amount of tranquillizers or sleeping pills helps me close my eyes. I've already seen the psychologist, who prescribed me a regular treatment. He told me, 'You've got to walk at least five minutes every day, and then you'll get better.' But I didn't get better, even after my husband tried to give me a stable environment.

Dreams never visit me. I just stay awake and fearful, waiting for evil. I remain awake every day, hoping to dream of my children. But maybe my daughter Rehab is angry with me and doesn't want to visit me in my dreams. She had wanted us to leave. [*She cries. The sound of the shelling reaches us, maybe from the post office in the direction of the Sofitel, followed by the response from the Sofitel itself to the place where the shell came from. Ezzeya screams and jumps up from where she is. She wants to run away, and the women try to calm her down. One of the women says, 'That shell was shot by the Hassem regiment* [63] *from the al-Ashbat towards the Sofitel.' Ezzeya grows angry, 'And so what? They're shooting back and our houses are in the middle.' She mumbles, choking on her words. I tell her, 'Drink some water, and you'll feel a little better.' She has some and quiets down.*]

I don't know what happens to me when I hear those sounds. Probably because they are the sounds of death. I tell myself that right now someone somewhere is being

63   Regiment of the Salafi resistance in Taiz.

killed in this city, a family is being wiped out. No sedatives, or visits to the doctor can make me come to terms with my tragedy, nothing. When I hear the sound of the shelling, I remember that moment. The bodies, and the pool of blood in our living room. The choked sighs of a beloved leaving this world. And my tense hands, moving without hope, in my son's head.

Ezzeya Abdo Mohammed Saleh

On Sunday, 10 May 2015, Houthi-Saleh militia shelled the house of Mansour Dahwan Huzam in the al-Ashhat neighbourhood in Taiz. Ezzeya's children were killed: Hamza Mansour Dahwan Huzam (11 years old), Rehab Mansour Dahwan Huzam (21 years old) and Rana Mansour Dahwan Huzam (16 years old). Her husband's first wife Najjiya Ali Mohammed Saeed (50 years old) and her son Mohammed Mansour Dahwan Huzam (17 years old) were killed as well. Ezzeya's neighbour Sabah Saeed Uthman al-Maqtari (45 years old), her daughter Hiba Fuad Ali Mohammed (17 years old), Ezzeya herself, and her daughter Marwa Mohammed Mansour Dahwan were all injured, as well as others.

NOT A SINGLE PHOTO SURVIVED

Everything is blurry in my head: thoughts, images, smells, memories. Sometimes I manage to make out faces, but I can never hear voices. Why have their voices disappeared? Why can't my memory preserve them? I can remember us laughing, but there's no sound. Our lives under one roof, our games as children, my mother's footsteps in the house, my little brother Hammudi getting up to no good, us sitting together at lunch with my brother Saddam, my sister Mariya and their families. Everything has now transformed into a distant past, one separated by walls of rubble, smoke, and war.

The day before, it was pouring, and the city streets were wet. The scent of soil mixed with fresh rainfall brought me joy. But you only remember happiness once it's gone, and all that's left behind is a bitterness that twists your insides. I went back home at night, and my family members were still up as usual. I spoke with my mother, who said she was going to travel in the morning and that she'd leave me all the family documents along with our property papers and those belonging to some villagers who'd left their deeds with my grandfather. My mother was terrified of the roaring bombs. I tried to calm her down and gave her a kiss. Afterwards I went back to the living room, still filled by the pleasant feeling the rain had given me. I slept without dreaming, like a child that hadn't slept for a long time.

At 5.45 a.m. on 11 May, during the first year of the war, I was jolted awake by the ground shaking beneath me. The ground swallowed everything atop it: people, walls, furniture, photos and even smells. I didn't hear the sound of the crashing missile – warning that catastrophe was coming – and so didn't have enough time to save my family. When a missile targets your house, you don't hear it coming, because the sound is too quick for your ears to catch it. What I do remember well is the ground shaking and eating up our house and twelve others in the al-Dehi neighbourhood. I remained conscious for a few minutes, but then began to choke on the gases released by the missile. The smoke was yellow; it smelt odd. Months after inhaling this gas, I'm still ill. My friend told me later on that the missile they used has been outlawed internationally. When I came to about an hour later, I took a look around. [*His voice breaks.*]

Our home had been flattened. Only the outside columns supporting the foundations were still there and the wall of the room I had been sleeping in was hanging loose. The rooms of the house had collapsed into a large hole that swallowed up debris, stones, and the limbs of my family. Scattered noise, neighbourhood children screaming, other people collecting items from our destroyed home. The Civil Defence Authority cars didn't come to save my family, and neither did the rescue vehicles belonging to the resistance or the militia. Just neighbours who pulled out the limbs of my family from the rubble, and informed me they'd found my sister Asmahan three buildings away, alive. I thought to myself, they must just be trying to give me hope – I mean, how could my sister with a heart condition survive while she was asleep in the same room as my other siblings? But when they confirmed that she was really alive, I cried with joy. At the same time, I observed the neighbourhood men, stunned, while they pulled out severed hands and mangled bodies. They found half of Saddam's body in the neighbourhood next over. They kept on pulling out more and more, and burying what they found. [*He walks on the rubble of what was his house, moving a rock to sit on. A burnt rug comes into view from underneath.*]

Since that day, I can no longer sleep. I lie down afraid; I'm endlessly falling down stairs. I see walls standing, the faces of my family looking at me from behind. And when I do surrender to sleep, something shakes me violently awake – something like an earthquake, consuming everything. So I keep chasing after sleep in the many houses I've lived in since the death of my family and destruction of our home. Sometimes I think of their final dreams. Or were they nightmares? What were they about, did they warn them of what was to come? I think of the moment they died – were they jolted awake like me or did they not wake up at all? Did death take them by surprise while they were sleeping, dreaming away, or did they look death in the eye as their bodies were torn in two?

The Coalition planes murdered my family. Their leaders haven't even bothered to apologize or acknowledge what they've done. To them, it was simply collateral damage; our blood is cheap, no one will ask after us. They didn't say, 'Sorry, Yassin, for killing your family, it wasn't intentional, but you know, it was just an unfortunate coincidence that the missile fell on your house.' But it wasn't just an unfortunate coincidence, Bushra, there aren't any barracks in front of our house or any military bases for the militia. The closest thing is a Houthi base more than a kilometre away. International law specifies this in wars – I've studied the law, and I know it well. Our neighbourhood was safe; people from close-by areas would seek refuge here. But Coalition planes don't distinguish between civilian and military targets. I always think about the pilot who dropped the missile on our house – does he have a family? Can he sleep at night? Did he think about killing innocent people before pressing the button? Did he have any regrets when he found out he'd murdered my family?

After the massacre of my family, I keep watching videos of the Coalition's military operations in our country. I lean in close to the images and scrutinize them. How the plane moves before taking off from Saudi Arabia to its targets in Yemen. I watch their modern devices that can detect even the face of a person as he walks down the street, and I wonder, what did my family do to deserve such a fate? I remember meeting one of the leaders of the Yemeni Islah party in the city. He was bragging about how they had been giving the Coalition the coordinates. Bragging about murder is horrific – have they no conscience at all? One day one of the resistance leaders in Taiz called me to offer his condolences. My entire family had supported the resistance against the militia. The leader of the resistance was angry about my family's murder, saying that they'd compensate me. I said, 'Getting compensation for our home is our right, but how will you compensate me for the death of my family? Will you bring them back to life?' He fell silent.

There was really nothing he could have said. Nothing will make up for my loss. Words of condolence lose their meaning. If it hadn't been for my friends, I would have lost my mind long ago. Can you imagine it? An entire family, wiped out. They didn't leave anything for me to remember them by, no smell of them, no pictures of them, for me to convince myself that they actually walked this earth. No personal documents. They burnt everything – not a single photo survived the tragedy. I often dream of my mother, but she never speaks to me. She smiles and carries on with whatever she's doing. I touch her face, but she disappears and I wake up, my own face wet with tears. I dream of my brother Saddam, remembering how he'd pick me up from school. I remember our chats and his advice, how we'd sit in the bookshop, watching people walk by. I restored the bookshop after the militia burnt it down; I want to keep the memories of my brother alive. I sit there for hours on end, lost in imaginary conversations with him, but such attempts to save my memory leave me exhausted.

I've lost my family and don't have a single photo of them, not a single photo that I can slip into my wallet and remember that I had a family once. A photo for me to look at, on those sleepless nights I spend searching through the rubble of our house for the life that I once had.

Yassin Abdelqawi Saleh al-Jabri

At 5.45 a.m. on Sunday, 11 May 2015, Arab Coalition planes bombed Yassin Abdelqawi Saleh al-Jabri's home in the al-Dehi neighbourhood of Taiz. His mother was killed. His brother Saddam Abdelqawi Saleh al-Jabri and Saddam's wife Amal, along with their children, Malak Saddam Abdelqawi Saleh al-Jabri (3 years old) and Abdelqawi Saddam Abdelqawi Saleh al-Jabri (5 years old), were all killed. Yassin's sister Marya Abdelqawi Saleh al-Jabri and her children, Hind (2 years old) and Hayam (4 years old), were also killed. Yassin's brother Ahmad Abdelqawi Saleh al-Jabri (12 years old) and his brother Abdallah Abdelqawi Saleh al-Jabri (2 years old) were also killed. Yassin's neighbour Amira Amin al-Tayyar (30 years old), a little girl Ranya al-Dahee, a little boy Rakaan al-Shareehe, and a teacher Ahmad Yahya were also all killed.

FOR REHAM BADR

We should have been celebrating the publication of this book together, blocking our ears from the whistling of missiles and the booming of air raids; the backdrop of death. We wouldn't think about the war going on outside. We'd meet our friends who'd helped us out, and get together like we used to in happier times, looking back fondly on old memories under the roofs of houses where we'd once felt safe. But you're not here. The war killed you like it killed thousands of innocents in this grief-stricken country.

Who knew, even in my worst nightmares, that I'd be writing about you in this book – the one you waited so long for – as a victim, not as a friend. You who had documented so many victims of war in this city, wiping away the tears of their loved ones with your gentle touch. Let me begin with a particularly pressing, vivid memory: my last memory of us together, crossing the muddy streets of this city, walking over the rubble of abandoned houses, listening to the sorrows of those present about those absent, us knocking on the closed doors of bereaved mothers waiting for their children who would never return.

You spoke at that time about the memory of horror in the city, lives forgotten, lives known only to sensitive souls like yours, Reham. You spoke of other victims who'd left their homes for fear of being bombed, not knowing as they shut their doors that they would never see their children again. You spoke of your neighbour who lost his sons and left the city, then the country too, to get as far away as possible, hoping to forget; of the mother who died giving birth because she couldn't get oxygen; of the young man who lost his mind after his friends were murdered. You spoke to me of those disabled by war in the backstreets of the old city; wounded individuals coming back from the front limbless, heavy with disappointment, their wounds rotting, without realizing who they'd been fighting for. You spoke to me about what the war did to the good citizens of this city after years of suffering, about the city's daily toil during the blockade, and how you'd hike up Mount Taluq to bring food to the affected families. When a man sobbed in front of his shop for his murdered children, you asked me how I would write all this pain – but you're no longer here for me to answer that. The war has killed you and left me perpetually wordless, staring into your absence.

Rest in peace, my friend.

Bushra al-Maqtari

At noon, Thursday, 8 February 2018, Reham Badr Abdel Waseea al-Dhabhani (32 years old) was killed along with her friend Ma'maoun al-Shar'abi, by a Houthi militia shell in the eastern area of the city of Taiz. At the time, they had both been distributing aid to families under the blockade. Reham was a Yemeni activist, founder of a humanitarian relief initiative in Taiz, and an inspector with NCIAVHR, National Commission to Investigate Alleged Violations of Human Rights in Yemen.

A LIST OF VICTIMS, IN BRIEF

In addition to the victims mentioned in the preceding accounts, this list covers the period between 26 March 2015 and 29 September 2017. It was largely created through my own research, with confirmation from the families of the victims. It is partly based on reports from international organizations including Amnesty International, and also such local organizations as the National Commission to Investigate Alleged Violations to Human Rights (www.nciye.org) and Mwatana for Human Rights (www.mwatana.org.en).

26 March 2015: Sanaa, Beni al-Harith, Beni Hawat. Air strike by the Arab Coalition (henceforth the 'Coalition') on a residential building on al-Matar Street kills 21 civilians.

30 March 2015: Hajjah, al-Mazraq IDP Camp. Air strike by the Coalition leads to death of 29 civilians.

31 March 2015: Aden, Khormaksar. Nine civilians died after artillery bombardment by Houthi-Saleh militia.

31 March 2015: Yarim at Ibb, Kitab. Air strike by the Coalition on two petrol stations and a gas truck kills 14 civilians.

1 April 2015: al-Hudaydah, Thabit Brothers Dairy. Air raid on the dairy by the Coalition kills 15 workers and injures several others.

3 April 2015: Sanaa, Beni Matar. Air strike by the Coalition on the village of Hajr Ukaish kills 10 civilians.

11 April 2015: Taiz, Mawiya district, al-Duhra village. Coalition air raid leads to death of 12 civilians, including 7 children and 3 women.

18 April 2015: Aden, al-Mu'ala, Konica building. Death of Sabrine Mohammad Ali by a Houthi-Saleh militia sniper.

20 April 2015: Taiz, al-Mudhaffar district. Death of Dr Abdulhalim al-Asbahi by a Houthi-Saleh militia sniper.

21 April 2015: Ibb, al-Dalil, Samara mountain pass. Coalition air raid on a mountain bridge kills 30 civilians.

26 April 2015: Ibb, al-Makhadir district, Dalil Bridge. Air raid on Dalil Bridge by the Coalition kills 22 civilians.

27 April 2015: Aden, Crater, Qutay', al-Ma'rib Street. Air strike by the Coalition on the apartment of the al-Tayyeb family, death of 4 family members: Younes Qassem Mohammad al-Tayyeb (53 years old), Bushra Qassem Ghulam Hussein (37 years old), Ihab Qassem Mohammad al-Tayyeb (42 years old) and Qassem Younes Qassem Mohammad al-Tayyeb (4 years old).

1 May 2015: Sanaa, Shu'ub district, Sa'wan. Air strike by the Coalition on an apartment in the Bab Sha'ab neighbourhood kills 17 civilians.

1 May 2015: Aden, Dar Sa'ad district. Haifa Malik al-Zuqari, an activist, dies by the bullet of a Houthi-Saleh militia sniper.

5 May 2015: Sa'dah, Sahar district. Air strike by the Coalition on the village of al-Dhubian leads to death of 8 civilians from one family.

7 May 2015: Taiz, al-Mudhaffar district. Khadijah Ahmad Abdulghani (15 years old) dies from shots fired by Houthi-Saleh militia.

11 May 2015: Taiz, al-Mudhaffar district. Air raid on al-Sunna mosque by the Coalition kills 5 civilians.

12 May 2015: al-Hudaydah, Zabid district, Main Street. Coalition air raid kills 42 civilians, including 9 children and 4 women.

27 May 2015: Taiz, Dimna Khadir district. Air strike by the Coalition on a petrol station in the al-Rahida area kills 18 civilians.

13 June 2015: Old City of Sanaa, al-Qasimi. Coalition air raid kills 5 civilians, including a child and a woman.

13 June 2015: Sanaa, al-Saba'in district. Coalition air strike in the Beit Ma'yad area kills 10 civilians.

16 June 2015: Lahij, Tur al-Bahah district. Coalition air strike on a car in the Khabt al-Rajaa area kills 11 civilians.

1 July 2015: Taiz, al-Qahira district, al Hawban. Coalition air strike on an apartment in the village of al-Najdin results in the death of 4 civilians from one family.

2 July 2015: Sa'dah, Sahar district, al-Talh area. Air strike by the Coalition on al-Ziraa neighbourhood kills 5 civilians.

12 July 2015: Sanaa, Shu'ub district, Sa'wan. Coalition air raid on the eastern working-class district kills 23 civilians.

20 July 2015: al-Dhalea', Qa'taba. Coalition air raid kills 5 civilians, including 2 children.

24 July 2015: Taiz, al-Mokha district. Air strike by the Coalition on a housing estate belonging to the employees of an electricity company kills 65 civilians, including 14 children and 13 women, and leaves several injured.

1 August 2015: Lahij, Tuban district, al-Hamra village. Air strike by the Coalition on the village of al-Hamra kills 8 civilians, including 2 children and 3 women.

5 August 2015: Taiz, al-Qahira district, Haud-al-Ashraf neighbourhood. Air strike by the Coalition on the al-Qimma ballroom kills 6 civilians from one family.

8 August 2015: Ibb, al-Radma district, Shar'a village Coalition air raid kills 7 civilians, including 3 children and 2 women.

8 August 2015: Taiz, al-Qahira district, al-Owaady Street. Three civilians are killed after being hit by a Houthi-Saleh militia grenade.

13 August 2015: Taiz, al-Qahira district, Wadi Madam. Five civilians are killed and others injured after being hit by a Houthi-Saleh militia grenade.

14 August 2015: Taiz, al-Qahira district, al-Mughtaribin. Death of 4 children, Marina Ahmad al-Samawi, Ilham Ahmad al-Samawi, Raghad Abdelkarim Abdullah and Aya Abdelkarim Abdullah, after being hit by a Houthi-Saleh militia shell.

17 August 2015: Ibb, Jibla district, Main Street. Coalition air raid on al-Qarama'a neighbourhood kills 5 civilians.

20 August 2015: Taiz, Salh district, Salh neighbourhood. Air strike by the Coalition on several houses kills 50 civilians, including 23 children and 12 women, and injures several others.

20 August 2015: Taiz, al-Qahira district, al-Kawthar neighbourhood. Four civilians killed and several injured after being hit by a Houthi-Saleh militia shell.

29 August 2015: Hajjah, Abs district, Beni Lahina village. Air strike by the Coalition on the Sham drinking water factory kills 17 civilians and injures several others.

30 August 2015: al-Bayda', Mukayras district, Mash'aba village. Air strike by the Coalition on the home of Mohammad al-Jarwi kills 10 civilians from one family.

5 September 2015: Sanaa, al-Saha'in district. Air strike by the Coalition on a residential building on al-Khamsin Street kills 7 civilians.

5 September 2015: Sanaa, al-Thawra district. Air strike by the Coalition on a residential building in al-Nahda district kills 9 civilians.

10 September 2015: Taiz, al-Mudhaffar district, Tabbat al-Aranih. Usama Ahmad, a child, killed by a Houthi-Saleh sniper.

15 September 2015: Taiz, Salh district, al-Thawra Public Hospital. Death of the child Amjad Abdulra'uf (15 years old) after being hit by a grenade from the Houthi-Saleh militia.

17 September 2015: Sanaa Old City, al-Fleihi neighbourhood. Coalition air raid kills 13 civilians, including 10 from the same family.

21 September 2015: Hajjah, al-Shaghadira, Dohr Abu Ter village. Air strike by the Coalition on the police station and a grocery shop kills 18 civilians, including children.

22 September 2015: Taiz, al-Qahira district, Haud-al-Ashraf neighbourhood. Death of Fathiya[64] (42 years old) and her

---

64 Due to the circumstances of the war it was impossible, in some cases, for me to contact the relatives of the victims to find out the full name and age of the deceased.

son Arafat (10 years old) by a grenade launched by Houthi-Saleh militia.

22 September 2015: Sanaa, Beni Hashish district. Air strike by the Coalition on the Martyr Abdullah Al Wazir School kills 3 civilians.

24 September 2015: Taiz, al-Qahira district, al-Tahrir neighbourhood. Eight civilians killed and several others injured after being hit by a Houthi-Saleh militia shell.

27 September 2015: Hajjah, Harad district, Zeilaa village. Air strike by the Coalition kills 18 civilians, 14 children and 4 women.

27 September 2015: Taiz, al-Mudhaffar district, al-Nuseiriyya. Civilians Radija Abdulaziz (59 years old), Rida Ali Ghanem (8 years old), Ithar Mohammad Ghanem (2 years old) killed after being hit by a Houthi-Saleh militia grenade.

28 September 2015: Taiz, Dhubab district, al-Wahijah village. Coalition air raid on a wedding party in the village kills 26 civilians, including 13 children and 12 women.

30 September 2015: Taiz, al-Mudhaffar district, al-Dehi neighbourhood. Mohammad Hassan Ali (13 years old) and Awad Said Ali (15 years old) killed after being hit by a Houthi-Saleh grenade.

1 October 2015: Taiz, al-Mudhaffar district, al-Ba'rara. Three civilians die after being hit by a Houthi-Saleh militia grenade.

5 October 2015: Taiz, Salh district, Thu'bat village. Salem Said Abdussamad (22 years old) and his son Mohammad Salem

Said Abdussamad (1 year old) are killed by a Houthi-Saleh militia sniper.

5 October 2015: Taiz, Sabr al-Mawadem district, al-Karifa. Aziza Mohammad Abdo (55 years old) and her two daughters Intissar Ali Ahmad (20 years old) and Ibtissam Ali Ahmad (22 years old) killed by the impact of a Houthi-Saleh militia grenade.

7 October 2015: Dhamar, Mayfa'at Ans, Sinhan village. Coalition air strike on a wedding reception kills 40 civilians, including 15 children and 14 women.

11 October 2015: Taiz, Salh district, al-Thawra Public Hospital. Two civilians, Wahib Mohammad Ghaleb al-Aghbari and Mohammad Khaled, killed by a Houthi-Saleh militia grenade.

14 October 2015: Taiz, Mawiya district. Coalition air raid on Ali Hamida's home leads to death of 11 members of his family.

14 October 2015: Taiz, al-Taiziyya district, Jabal al-Wa'sh. Afkar Qaed Murshid (19 years old) killed by a Houthi-Saleh militia sniper.

15 October 2015: Taiz, al-Mudhaffar district, al-Masbah neighbourhood. Naoual al-Shara'bi killed after being hit by a Houthi-Saleh militia grenade.

21 October 2015: Taiz, al-Qahira district, al-Dabu'a neighbourhood/al-Markazi neighbourhood/ 26 September Street. Thirteen civilians killed by Katyusha rockets fired by Houthi-Saleh militia: Rida Fahim Mohammad (19 years old), Amjad Marwan Abdullah (10 years old), Jalal Wajdi (15 years old), Wassem Ali Said (35 years old), Abdullah Ahmad al-Sama'i (50 years old), Ali Abdulwahid (45 years old), Nabil Mohammad Abdo (45 years old), Ammar Mohammad Abdullah (25 years old), Suhaim Mohammad Said al-Dahbali (27 years old), Samira Ahmad al-Shar'abi (18 years old), Sumaiyya Ahmad Ali (17 years old), Majid Abdulkhaleq Abdulmajid and a person of unknown identity.

22 October 2015: al-Hudaydah, Beit al-Faqih district, Ka'aban Island. Air strike by the Coalition on fishing boats in the vicinity of the island kills 42 civilians and injures several others.

22 October 2015: Taiz, al-Qahira district, al-Rawda neighbourhood. Two civilians, Abdo Maresh Hizaa (40 years old) and Badri Ali Ahmad (24 years old) are killed by a Houthi-Saleh militia shell.

22 October 2015: Taiz, al-Mudhaffar district, al-Dehi neighbourhood. Ismail Mohammad Ahmad (25 years old) and 'Alaa Abdo' Aqlan al-Qudsi (25 years old) are killed by a Houthi-Saleh militia grenade.

26 October 2015: Taiz, al-Qahira, al-Rauda. Abdullah Mohammad Ali Seif al-Azzi (14 years old) is killed by a Houthi-Saleh sniper.

29 October 2015: Taiz, Salh district, al-Hawban. Air strike by the Coalition on a bus carrying workers from the Hael Said An'am company kills 10 workers.

5 November 2015: Taiz, al-Mudhaffar district, Sina neighbourhood. Four civilians are killed by the impact of a Houthi-Saleh militia shell.

6 November 2015: Taiz, al-Qahira district, al-Jumhuri neighbourhood. Munif Abdulalim Bashar (40 years old) and his two children Muqbil Munif Abdulalim (11 years old) and Manar Munif Abdulalim (9 years old) are killed by a Houthi-Saleh militia shell.

7 November 2015: Taiz, al-Mudhaffar district, Sina neighbourhood. Mohammad Ryad Hassan (1 year old) killed by the explosion of a Houthi-Saleh militia grenade.

13 November 2015: al-Dhalea', Dimth al-Qadima. Ahmad Muhsin al-Sahifi is killed by a Houthi-Saleh militia grenade.

17 November 2015: al-Hudaydah, Bajil district. Professor Abdussalam al-Shumairi is killed and his 2 sons captured by Houthi-Saleh militia, who also blew up his apartment.

17 November 2015: Taiz, Salh district, al-Qasr roundabout. Ali Salim Ahmad (60 years old) dies at the hands of a Houthi-Saleh sniper.

19 November 2015: al-Hudaydah, al-Khokha. Coalition air strike on fishing boats results in the death of 15 fishermen including: Mastur Ali Ahmad Dobla Akram Hassan Ali Dobla, Adel Ali Khadem Hamami and Ammar Qaed Ja'man. Other fishermen disappeared and most likely drowned at sea: Mohammad Salman Ali Daublo, Mohammad Ali Ahmad Daublo, Qaed Ali Ja'man, Abdullah Ibrahim Mohammad Darwish, Mohammad Salman Mohammad Khudeishi, Ahmad Thabet Hassan Tari, Yasser Mohammad Qassem Farid, Said Ali Mohammad Darwish and Murshid Ahmad Hama.

19 November 2015: Taiz, Sabr al-Mawadem, al-Dim. Five civilians killed by a Houthi-Saleh grenade: Mahmud Hassan Abdullah Ali (55 years old), Ahlam Mohammad Hassan Abdullah Ali (29 years old), Iftikar Ahmad Hizaa Qassem (29 years old), Rama Talal Hassan Ali (3 years old) and Lutfi Mohammad Abdulbasset Hassan (1 year old).

20 November 2015: al-Mahwit. Ali 'Auda tortured to death in a Houthi-Saleh militia prison.

23 November 2015: al-Jauf, east of Jabal al-Lodh. Coalition air raid on a house kills a father and 8 other family members.

27 November 2015: Taiz, al-Mudhaffar district, al-Dehi neighbourhood. Qussai Ahmad al-Nahari (11 years old) killed by a Houthi-Saleh militia sniper.

28 November 2015: Taiz, al-Qahira district, al-Dabu'a neighbourhood. Nidaa Amin al-Salahi (10 years old) and another girl killed when a Houthi-Saleh militia grenade explodes and destroys a drinking-water tanker.

29 November 2015: Taiz, al-Mudhaffar district, al-Dehi neighbourhood. Abdullah Abdo al-Humairi is killed by a Houthi-Saleh sniper as he returns from a dialysis session.

30 November 2015: Taiz, al-Qahira district, al-Manakh neighbourhood. Nea'ma Abdullah Qa'ed al-Rimi (60 years old) is killed and her son Ammar al-Kuri is injured by a Houthi-Saleh militia grenade.

2 December 2015: Taiz, Salh district, al-Damgha neighbourhood. Adib Hammoud Mahdi al-Unsi is killed by a Houthi-Saleh militia sniper.

4 December 2015: Taiz, al-Mudhaffar district, al-Hassib. Rakan Abdullah Naji (8 years old) and Abdo Abdullah Abdo Ahmad (20 years old) are killed by a Houthi-Saleh militia sniper.

4 December 2015: Taiz, Salh, al-Damgha district. Safia Ahmad Said al-Marzuh (65 years old) is killed by a Houthi-Saleh sniper.

5 December 2015: Taiz, al-Misrakh, Arsh. Najla Abdulhamid al-Shuraihi and her sister Afaf Abdulhamid al-Shuraihi are killed by Houthi-Saleh militia shell.

7 December 2015: Taiz, al-Qahira district, Usaifira neighbourhood. Four civilians killed and several others injured by the impact of a Houthi-Saleh militia shell.

12 December 2015: al-Hudaydah, Port of al-Khokha. Coalition air raid on fishing boats kills 5 fishermen.

13 December 2015: Taiz, al-Mokha district. Air strike by the Coalition on a power station kills four civilians.

13 December 2015: Sa'dah, Dahian. Coalition air raid on Ali Raqea's home kills three family members.

13 December 2015: Lahij, al-Qabbaita, al-Haidin. Coalition air raid on a taxi rank kills 6 civilians and injures several others.

13 December 2015: Hajjah, Harad district, al-Hijawira. Coalition air strike kills 11 civilians and injures several people.

15 December 2015: Hajjah, Harad district, Beni al-Haddad village. Coalition air strike kills 10 civilians and injures several people.

15 December 2015: Taiz, al-Misrakh district, al-Aqrud. Mohammad Abdo Abbas (12 years old) dies after the explosion of a mine laid by Houthi-Saleh militia.

15 December 2015: Taiz, al-Mudhaffar district, Sha'ab Salit neighbourhood. Khalil Mohammad Ahmad al-Kibash is killed by the impact of a Houthi-Saleh militia shell.

15 December 2015: Taiz, Salh district, al-Damgha neighbourhood. Budur Amin Salih Yahya al-Maghrami (8 years old) is killed by the impact of a Houthi-Saleh militia shell.

18 December 2015: Sa'dah, al-Safra, Kanna. Air strike by the Coalition on the home of Abdullah al-Matari kills 4 of his family members; this air strike was followed by another on rescue workers at the site, which killed 10 others.

20 December 2015: Taiz, al-Qahira district, al-Kawthar mosque neighbourhood. Jalal Hizaa al-Asbahi (45 years old) killed by Houthi-Saleh militia shell that hit his home.

23 December 2015: Sa'dah, Kitaf district, Wadi Amlah. Air strike by the Coalition on the village of al-Khanaq kills 19 members of Hammoud Hamid al-Azzi's family; all the dead were civilians.

23 December 2015: Taiz, al-Mudhaffar district, al-Dehi neighbourhood. Hizaa Ali Abdulhafiz (29 years old) killed by a Houthi-Saleh militia sniper.

24 December 2015: al-Hudaydah, al-Khokha, al-Hayma port. Coalition air strike kills 2 civilians and injures several others.

24 December 2015: Lahij, Balah. Two children die after a mine laid by Houthi-Saleh militia explodes.

25 December 2015: Taiz, al-Misrakh district. Four members of Abdurrahman al-Hashidi's family are killed by the explosion of a mine laid by Houthi-Saleh militia.
28 December 2015: Ma'rib, Mount Hailan. Nada al-Awadi (10 years old) dies after she is hit by a Houthi-Saleh militia grenade.

29 December 2015: Taiz, al-Mudhaffar district, al-Nuseiriyya
Radia Abdulaziz al-Daba'i is killed by a Houthi-Saleh militia shell.

31 December 2015: Taiz, Salh district, al-Thawra Public Hospital. Death of Tahani Ali Mohammad's newborn daughter due to lack of oxygen as a result of the blockade imposed on the city by Houthi-Saleh militia.

1 January 2016: Taiz, al-Taiziyya district, al-Rahida. Coalition air strike on Hamra area kills Najib Zawet and his children.

1 January 2016: Taiz, Salh district, al-Thawra Public Hospital. Death of the newly born daughter of Nasser Ahmad due to lack of oxygen as a result of the blockade imposed on the city by Houthi-Saleh militia.

2 January 2016: Taiz, Salh district, Thu'bat neighbourhood/ Sina/Kahlan. Death of Zainab Ahmad (50 years old) in Sina, Amina Ali (75 years old) in Thu'bat and Ghada Ahmad Qaed (25 years old) in the village of Kahlan by the impact of grenades of Houthi-Saleh militia.

2 January 2016: Taiz, Sarar. Houthi militia execute 3 prisoners; the executed were members of the anti-Houthi resistance.

3 January 2016: Taiz, Salh district, al-Thawra Hospital. Eatissam Abdulaziz Hamid Mohammad, a young girl, dies from lack of oxygen due to the blockade imposed on the city by Houthi-Saleh militia.

5 January 2016: Taiz, al-Mudhaffar district, al-Nuseiriyya. Husn Farhan Hamid (45 years old) and Younes Daghesh Mohammad (4 years old) killed during bombing by Houthi-Saleh militia.

6 January 2016: Sanaa, Mo'ein. A fission bomb dropped by the Coalition kills a civilian and injures several people others.

9 January 2016: Taiz, al-A'abus district, al-Dhabi village. Rahma Ali Hael is killed by a Houthi-Saleh sniper.

10 January 2016: Taiz, al-Qahira district, al-Masbah neighbourhood. Two civilians are killed by the impact of a Houthi-Saleh militia shell.

10 January 2016: Ma'rib, Majzar district. Two civilians die after a mine laid by Houthi-Saleh militia explodes.

11 January 2016: Taiz, Salh district, al-Thawra Public Hospital Death of Rasha Hizaa's newborn son and Alouf Mohammad's twin daughters due to lack of oxygen as a result of the blockade imposed on the city by Houthi-Saleh militia.

13 January 2016: Sanaa, Bilad al-Rus district. Air strike by the Coalition on the Jarif thermal baths kills 10 civilians and injures several others.

14 January 2016: Ma'rib, Sirwah. Air strike by the Coalition on the ancient temple of Sirwah partially destroys the temple.

15 January 2016: Taiz, al-Qahira district, al-Masbah. Raed Ali Ali (20 years old) dies from the explosion of a Katyusha rocket fired by Houthi-Saleh militia.

17 January 2016: Sanaa, Bilad al-Rus district. Coalition air raid on the Jarif thermal baths kills several civilians, including the journalist al-Miqdad Mohammad Ali Madjali, correspondent for the Voice of America.

17 January 2016: Taiz, al-Mudhaffar district, al-Dehi neighbourhood. Hamid Hussein al-Shumairi (50 years old) and Hamid Abduljalil al-Shumairi (70 years old) killed by a Houthi-Saleh militia grenade.

17 January 2016: Taiz, Salh district, al-Jahmilia al-Sufla. Death of Mohammad Abdullah Abdo (12 years old) after he is shot by a Houthi-Saleh sniper.

19 January 2016: Taiz, al-Taiziyya district, al-Harir. Air raid on a school by the Coalition kills 7 students.

20 January 2016: al-Dhalea', Damth. Houthi militia blows up the homes of Qaed Abu Mulham al-Sajjadi and Ahmad al-Ghazzi.

21 January 2016: al-Hudaydah, Ra's Issa. Air strike by the Coalition on an oil refinery kills 13 employees, including Walid Khaled Hamid, Saghir Jabber Ahmad, Ibrahim Hussein Mukarrash, Bassem Qatashi, Anwar Abdulhamid Kweik and Abdo Mohammad Sajjid, as well as 7 oil truck drivers.

21 January 2016: Sa'dah, Dahian, Majez district. Coalition air strike on an ambulance and paramedics kills 15 civilians, including Hashem Mohammad al-H'Amran, cameraman for the Almasira Media Network.

23 January 2016: al-Dhalea', Ya'is. A woman and her child are killed by a Houthi-Saleh sniper.

23 January 2016: Sanaa, Airport Road, Wadi Ahmad neighbourhood. Ahmad Hassan Abdulbaqi dies from the gaseous fumes released after an air strike by the Coalition on a chloride factory.

27 January 2016: Taiz, al-Qahira district, al-Kawthar neighbourhood. Four civilians, including 3 children, are killed by a Houthi-Saleh militia shell: Rammah Adel Taha (13 years old), Suhail Samir Thabet (13 years old), Mohammad Wassim Mohammad (6 years old) and Abubakr Mansur al-Abassi (25 years old).

28 January 2016: Taiz, Salh district, al-Shammasi. Akram Ali Makrad (13 years old) dies from the explosion of a Houthi-Saleh militia grenade.

30 January 2016: Dhamar. Munif al-Jabari, an inmate at a prison camp run by Houthi militia, is tortured to death.

31 January 2016: Taiz, Salh district, Thu'bat. Two civilians killed by the explosion of a Houthi-Saleh militia Katyusha rocket.

1 February 2016: Ibb, al-Hazm district, al-Qatib. Houthi militia execute Talal Hamid Abdo Qassem in front of his family.

1 February 2016: Taiz, al-Qahira district, Wadi al-Qadi. Amal Yassin al-Maqtari (18 years old) is killed by a Houthi-Saleh militia sniper.

2 February 2016: 'Amran, 'Amran cement factory. Coalition air raid on the factory kills 15 workers and injures several others.

2 February 2016: Hajjah, Harad. Coalition air strike kills 10 civilians.
2 February 2016: Dhamar, Jebel al-Sharq district. Coalition air raid on local police headquarters kills 2 civilians.

2 February 2016: Sanaa, Nihm district, Beni Hajjil. Air strike by the Coalition on the village of Beni Hajjil kills a child and injures several others.

2 February 2016: al-Hudaydah, district Administration Building. Coalition air raid on the district administration building kills 1 and injures several others.

2 February 2016: Taiz, al-Mudhaffar district, al-Nuseiriyya. Four civilians are killed due to the impact of a Houthi-Saleh militia shell.

3 February 2016: Sanaa, Nihm district, Sadd. Coalition air strike on a car kills 9 civilians, mostly women and children.

3 February 2016: Taiz, al-Misrakh district. Warda Abdulwasea is shot to death by a Houthi-Saleh militia sniper.

4 February 2016: Hajjah, Harad district, Beni al-Haddad. Coalition air raid on a residential building kills 5 civilians.

4 February 2016: al-Jauf, junction between al-Jauf and Ma'rib Death of a father and his son following the explosion of a mine laid by Houthi-Saleh militia.

12 February 2016: Taiz, al-Qahira district, al-Salkhana. Two civilians, including a child, are killed and several more injured as a result of shelling by Houthi-Saleh militia.

13 February 2016: Taiz, al-Mudhaffar district. Troops of the resistance kill Marwan al-Junaid (15 years old).

14 February 2016: Sanaa, Shu'ub district, Sheraton neighbourhood. Air strike by the Coalition on al-Wassabi Tailoring kills 11 civilians.

14 February 2016: Sa'dah, Haidan, Maran. Air strike by the Coalition kills a civilian and leaves several others injured.

14 February 2016: Taiz, al-Taiziyya, al-Janad. Air strike by the Coalition leaves the driver of a bulldozer dead.

14 February 2016: Kaukaban, al-Mouhin. Coalition air raid kills 10 civilians and injures several others.

15 February 2016: Taiz, al-Misrakh district, Kahlan Three children are killed by a Houthi-Saleh militia shell: Mohammad Amin Qahtan, Osama Abdulwasea Ali Ahmad and Jawad Abduljalil Ibrahim.

15 February 2016: al-Hudaydah, Sardad Valley. Air strike by the Coalition on a field kills 4 farmers.

16 February 2016: Taiz, al-Mudhaffar district, al-Hassib neighbourhood. Ahmad al-Shaibani, cameraman for the al-Yemen station, is killed by a Houthi-Saleh militia sniper.

17 February 2016: Sanaa, Nihm district, Uzlat neighbourhood, al-Na'imat village. Taresh Mohammad Ali al-Na'imi's home is destroyed by five Coalition rockets; 13 civilians from his immediate family and other relatives are killed: Ali Yahya Saleh al-Dahmashi (50 years old), Aziza Mohammad Ali Seif al-Na'imi (50 years old), Taresh Zahim Taresh Mohammad Ali al-Na'imi (12 years old), Ahmad Zahim Taresh Mohammad Ali al-Na'imi (11 years old), Hajar Zahim Taresh Mohammad Ali al-Na'imi (7 years old), Hafezullah Ahmad Salih al-Sadi al-Na'imi (16 years old), Balkis Abdulwali Ali Hadjia al-Na'imi (9 years old), Amal Abdulwali Ali Hadija al-Na'imi (10 years old), Mohammad Abdulwali Ali Hadija al-Na'imi (6 years old), Ashraa Ali Yahya Salih al-Dahmashi (16 years old), Abraj Amir Ali Yahya al-Dahmashi (16 years old), Ali Taleb Ali Hadija al-Na'imi (6 years old) and Salih Taleb Hadija al-Na'imi (5 years old).

17 February 2016: Taiz, al-Mudhaffar district, Sina. Three children are killed by the explosion of a Houthi-Saleh militia grenade: Ru'a Nabil, Malak Nabil and Khaula Fadel.

18 February 2016: Sa'dah, Munabbih district. Air strike by the Coalition on a car on the highway kills 2 civilians.

18 February 2016: al-Jauf, Aqaba district, Birt al-Marashi. Air strike by the Coalition on a residential building in the Milfaj area kills 2 civilians.

18 February 2016: al-Jauf, Birt al-Anan. Air strike by the Coalition on a gas-filled transporter kills 2 civilians.

19 February 2016: Taiz, al-Mudhaffar district, al-Darba neighbourhood. Two children, Raidan Ma'mun and Besher Hamza, are killed by a Houthi-Saleh militia shell.

19 February 2016: Sanaa, Nihm district, Buran. Coalition air strike on al-Haul al-Sharqi village kills 2 civilians.

20 February 2016: Lahij, al-Shuraija. Houthi militia executes Colonel Zaid Ahmad al-Jadri.

21 February 2016: Sanaa, Beni Dahyan. Coalition air strike on a car kills 6 civilians, all members of one family.

21 February 2016: Sa'dah, al-Zahir border area. Coalition air strike on Ghafira area kills 20 civilians, including women and children.

22 February 2016: Sanaa, Nihm district. Coalition air strike on two homes in Amlah kills 3 bystanders.

22 February 2016: al-Jauf, Wadi al-Matma, Wadi Kharid. Coalition air strike on three trucks kills 3 civilians.

25 February 2016: Ma'rib, Sirwah district. Coalition air strike on a home kills 3 civilians.

25 February 2016: Taiz, Dimnat Khadir district. Coalition air raid kills 4 civilians.

25 February 2016: Sanaa, al-Saba'in, Beit Ma'yad. Coalition air strike on Mohammad al-Raidi's house kills 3 civilians, including a baby.

27 February 2016: Sanaa, Nihm district, Khalqa Market. Coalition air raid kills 25 civilians and leaves several others injured.

27 February 2016: Taiz, al-Misrakh district, al-Shaqab. A young girl, Ghadir Abdulwahid (8 years old), is shot to death by a Houthi-Saleh militia sniper.

27 February 2016: Taiz, Salh district, Sha'ab Daba neighbourhood. Wael Abdullah Ahmad (22 years old) and Abedrabbo Mohammad Haidara (60 years old) are killed by the explosion of a Houthi-Saleh militia grenade.

1 March 2016: Sanaa, al-Haima al-Dakhiliyyah district. Coalition air strike on Beni Youssef School kills 8 civilians.

9 March 2016: Shabwah, Aqbat Bihan. Coalition air strike on a Hilux vehicle kills 3 civilians.

9 March 2016: al-Jauf, al-Humaydat district. Coalition air strike on a taxi kills 3 civilians and injures several others.

11 March 2016: Taiz, Salh district, Sina. Three civilians are killed when they are hit by a Houthi-Saleh militia shell.

12 March 2016: Sanaa, Khawlan al-Tiyal district. Coalition air strike on a car in Beni Jabar al-Makhruq area kills 5 civilians from the same family, including a woman and 3 children.

13 March 2016: Taiz, al-Mudhaffar district. Two children, Mohammad Mahyub Ali Abdullah and Muhannad Fadel Haidar Youssef, are killed when a Houthi-Saleh militia grenade explodes.

15 March 2016: Hajjah, Mustab'a. Coalition air strike on a Thursday market kills 131 civilians and wounds 86 others.

17 March 2016: Taiz, al-Taiziyya district. Coalition air strike on homes in Hadhran area kills a mother and her 2 children.

17 March 2016: Taiz al-Mudhaffar district, al-Darba. Two civilians, including a woman, are killed by the explosion of a Houthi-Saleh militia shell.

17 March 2016: Taiz, al-Qahira district, al-Ikhwa neighbourhood. Two civilians are killed after a Katyusha rocket fired by Houthi-Saleh militia hits them and explodes.

18 March 2016: Taiz, al-Mudhaffar district, al-Zanqal neighbourhood. The body of Ahmad Abdulhamid al-Shumairy is found after his assassination by Houthi-Saleh militia six months earlier.

18 March 2016: al-Hudaydah. Execution of Ahmad Baqi by the Houthis in front of his shop after he refuses to pay the war tax.[65]

19 March 2016: Taiz, al-Qahira district, 26 September Street. Seven civilians are killed by the blast of a Katyusha rocket

---

65   Translator's note: civilians are required to pay tax to the different warring parties, depending on who controls the area they live in.

fired by Houthi-Saleh militia.

20 March 2016: Taiz, Sabr al-Mawadem district, al-Dabab. Air raid by Coalition, 4 women and 2 children killed.

21 March 2016: al-Jauf, al-Mutun district. Coalition air strike on two vans loaded with gas and food kills 4 civilians.

21 March 2016: al-Jauf, al-Mutun Monday market. Coalition air strike on Dahouq Institute kills 7 civilians.

21 March 2016: Taiz, al-Waze'iya. Two civilians are killed and several others injured by two Houthi-Saleh militia rockets.

22 March 2016: Taiz, Sabr al-Mawadem district, al-Maqhaya. Five civilians die after a mine laid by Houthi-Saleh militia explodes under a bus.

23 March 2016: al-Hudaydah, al-Hujaila district. Coalition air raid kills 4 civilians.

25 March 2016: Taiz, Jabal Habashi district, Bilad al-Wafi neighbourhood. Coalition air raid on the village of Tabisha'a hits the home of Fikri Mohammad al-Dirgham, killing him and 11 of his family members.

31 March 2016: Taiz, Maqbana district, al-Akhlud al-Uqma. Coalition air strike on a home in al-Akhlud village kills 11 civilians.

3 April 2016: Ma'rib, al-Hay'a Hospital. Six civilians, including doctors, die after a Houthi-Saleh militia shell hits the hospital.

8 April 2016: Taiz, al-Waze'iya. Coalition air strike on two vehicles transporting displaced individuals kills 6 civilians and injures several others.

8 April 2016: Taiz, Salh district, Sha'ab Daba neighbourhood. Wael Abdullah Ahmad (22 years old) and Abed Rabbo Mohammad Haidara (50 years old) are killed by a Houthi-Saleh militia grenade.

13 April 2016: Shabwah, Usailan district, al-Hama village. Three children die after a Houthi-Saleh militia shell hits their village.

19 April 2016: Sanaa, Nihm district, Mahalli. Coalition air strike on the home of Mohammad Zayed al-Quhaili kills 7 family members.

22 April 2016: Hajjah, Midi district. Ahmad Assad, a member of the Armed Forces Ceasefire Committee, is killed by a Houthi-Saleh militia shell.

23 April 2016: Taiz, al-Taiziyya district, al-Rabie'i Street. A mine laid by Houthi-Saleh militia blows up 10 civilians (including a woman and 2 children): Mohammad Khaled Sultan (18 years old), Munir Abdullah Mohammad (66 years old), Nu'am Thabet Ahmad (65 years old), Amin Abdo Shaker (52 years old), Hawwab Ahmad Ali Farea, Mahdi Sultan Salam (8 years old), Mohammad Amin al-Asbah, Ibrahim Hussein Abdullah (20 months old), Salah Omar Mohammad al-Najashi (22 years old) and Dalia Abdullah Nasser (25 years old).

25 April 2016: Aden, al-Mansura district. Religious extremists assassinate Omar Batawil (18 years old).

1 June 2016: Taiz, al-Qahira district, Freedom Square neighbourhood. Three civilians die and several are injured after Houthi-Saleh militia shelling.

3 June 2016: Taiz, al-Mudhaffar district, al-Bab al-Kabir. A Katyusha rocket fired by Houthi-Saleh militia hits the

Bab al-Kabir market, killing 8 civilians: Sami Abdo Ali (30 years old), Arzaq Jamil al-Wassabi (7 years old), Muqbil Murshid Ghaleb (60 years old), Hammada Mohammad al-Aubli (35 years old), Fakiha Ahmad Said Farea (55 years old), Mustafa Hammoud Mulhi (17 years old), Adel Ali Mohammad (18 years old) and Safia Ali Abadi (50 years old).

3 June 2016: Taiz, al-Qahira district, Jamal Street. A civilian is killed by a Katyusha rocket fired by Houthi-Saleh militia.

4 June 2016: Taiz, al-Mudhaffar district, al-Ba'rara. Two civilians are killed when a Howitzer shell fired by Houthi-Saleh militia explode near them.

6 June 2016: Taiz, al-Mudhaffar district, old airport. Impact of a Houthi-Saleh militia grenade on the house of Shauqi Ahmad results in the death of Asia Ahmad Mohammad (35 years old).

7 June 2016: Taiz, al-Qahira district, al-Shamasi neighbourhood. Houthi-Saleh militia shelling of the entrance to the Bara'im School, where internally displaced persons had found refuge, results in the death of Khadija Sultan Qaed (31 years old) and her children Bashir Sami Qaed (6 years old), Ahmad Sami Qaed (6 years old) and Sultan Sami Qaed (8 years old), and their neighbour Ahmad Mohammad Nasser (27 years old).

7 June 2016: Taiz, al-Mudhaffar district, Wadi al-Qadi. Haela Ali Naji and her daughter Assil Hael (2 years old) die after Houthi-Saleh militia bombing.

21 June 2016: Lahij, al-Qubbaita. Coalition air strike on a group of workers kills 7.

22 June 2016: Ibb, al-Nadira, Maulat al-Nadish village. Houthi-Saleh militia opens fire on villagers, killing 7: Akram al-Hanhana, Arafat al-Hanhana, Adib al-Juraidi, Mahir al-Juraidi, Mohammad Abduljalil Maimoun, Ahmad Abduljalil Maimoun and Issa al-Jabali.

24 June 2016: al-Jauf, al-Mutun. Coalition air strike on two vehicles belonging to units loyal to President Hadi kills 20 men.

26 June 2016: Lahij, al-Qubbaita. Coalition air strike on apartment building kills 2 women.

27 June 2016: Abyan, al-Mahfad district, al-Murtafea al-Qarara village. Coalition air strike on Badran Lash'ab Khamis Awad's home kills 8 from the same family: Badran Lash'ab Khamis Awad, Majda Mustafa Lash'ab Khamis (8 years old), Mujahid Mustafa Lash'ab Khamis (6 years old), Sumayya Mustafa Lash'ab Khamis Awad (4 years old), Safia Badran Lash'ab Khamis Awad (1 year old), Bushra Ali Lash'ab Khamis Awad (7 years old), the pregnant Aisha Abdullah Khamis Awad and Nour Nasser Ahmad Awad.

29 June 2016: Lahij, al-Qubbaita, al-Rama village. Three children die after a Houthi-Saleh militia shell hits their village.

5 July 2016: Ma'rib, al-Ziraa neighbourhood. A Houthi-Saleh militia shell explodes, killing 8 children: Youssef Abdulwahhab al-Samei, Mohammad Abdulwahhab al-Samei, Ibrahim Mohammad Abdo Mahyub, Abir Mohammad Abdo Mahyub, Bilal Qaed Dammaj, Saleh Abdullah al-Ahmadi, Aiman Hamid Mazkur and Badr Saleh Mahdi.

12 July 2016: al-Hudaydah, al-Khokha district. Coalition air strike on fishing centre in the Qutaba area kills 2 fishermen.

18 July 2016: Sanaa Central Prison. Bassam al-Salawi, who was kidnapped and imprisoned by Houthi-Saleh militia, dies.

18 July 2016: al-Hudaydah, Jabal al-Nar market. Coalition air raid on the market kills 4 civilians.

26 July 2016: Taiz, Mount Saber, al-Sarari village. Villagers kidnapped by resistance fighters; the village is set on fire and other residents are evicted.

3 August 2016: al-Bayda', Dhilmalajim district. Four tribal elders of the Omari clan, Sheikh Ahmad Saleh al-Omari, his son Sheikh Saleh Ahmad Saleh al-Omari, Sheikh Mohammad Ahmad al-Omari and Sheikh Saleh Salem, are executed by Houthi militia.

5 August 2016: Sa'dah, Baqem district. Coalition air strike on Salem al-Qaradi's car kills 3 civilians.

5 August 2016: Sanaa, Nihm district. Coalition air raid on the home of Zeid al-Faraj in the al-Mujawaha area kills 2 women.

5 August 2016: al-Jauf, al-Gheil. The journalist Mubarak al-Obadi is killed by a Houthi-Saleh militia grenade.

7 August 2016: Sanaa, Nihm district. Coalition air strike on Madid market kills 12 civilians and injures several others.

9 August 2016: Taiz, al-Waze'iya district. Eleven civilians, including 3 children, are killed after a mine laid by Houthi-Saleh militia explodes.

12 August 2016: Sa'dah, Baqem district. Coalition air strike on a home in the al-Hamaqi area kills 8 civilians.

12 August 2016: Sa'dah, al-Mutun district. Coalition air raid kills 3 civilians, including a woman.

13 August 2016: Sa'dah, Haidan district. Coalition air strike on Jumu'a Bin Fadel School kills 10 children.

15 August 2016: Hajjah, Harad district. Coalition air raid on the Abbas Hospital, run by Doctors Without Borders, kills 11 civilians and injures several others.

16 August 2016: Sanaa, Nihm district. Coalition air raid on the home of Sheikh Mohsen Assem kills 13 civilians, including Mohsen Mohammad Assem (65 years old), Mohammad Jamil Mohsen Assem (5 years old), Hajar Jamil Assem (18 months old), Riham Jamil Assem (10 years old), Aushem Hamir Qahqa (28 years old), Mina Naef Dahesh, Aman Naef Dahesh, Mabrouk Daifullah al-Hajj (35 years old) and Huda Ali Assem (35 years old).

27 August 2016: Taiz, al-Taiziyya district, Shar'ab Junction. Coalition air raid kills 7 civilians and injures several others.

2 September 2016: Sanaa, Arhab district. Coalition air strike on apartment building kills 10 civilians, including women and children.

2 September 2016: al-Hudaydah Cultural Centre. Coalition air strike kills a civilian.

16 September 2016: Sanaa, Khawlan al-Tayal. Coalition air strike kills 13 civilians and injures several others.

18 September 2016: al-Hudaydah. Four civilians, Salem Ghaleb Said Musharrea (5 years old), Jalmud Ahmad Shanini (50 years old), Awassa Mohammad Abdo (31 years old) and the pregnant Fattoum Sadek Durra, starve to death.

19 September 2016: al-Hudaydah, coastal strip villages. Five civilians, Wahib Mohammad Said Jalab (3 years old), Saleh Shaqi Abdo Barr (52 years old), Sobha Ismail Ward (4 years old), Ali Bakkar Jabali and Zahra Kaddaf Zanba'a (5 years old), starve to death.

21 September 2016: al-Jauf, al-Mutmana. Coalition air strike on al-Minsab village kills 16 civilians, mostly women and children.

24 September 2016: Ibb, Jableh Junction. Coalition air strike on the Mahyub al-Audi building kills 7 civilians, including 5 from one family: Mohammad Abdo al-Jama'i, Ruqayya Hassan Ali al-Jama'i, Abeer Mohammad Abdo al-Jama'i, Abdurrahim Mohammad Abdo al-Jama'i, Mohammad Salah al-Da'is and Diaa Salah al-Da'is.

30 September 2016: Sa'dah, Razeh district. Coalition air strike on car kills 5 civilians.

30 September 2016: Sa'dah, Shadaa district. Coalition air strike on a car kills 4 civilians.

2 October 2016: Taiz, Mokha district, Wahijah. Coalition air strike on fishing boats kills 3 fishermen.

4 October 2016: al-Jauf, al-Jauf al-Ali. Coalition air strike on the motorcade of Sheikh Abdullah Munif, head of the pacification committee, kills 3 civilians.

8 October 2016: Sanaa, al-Kubra Hall. Coalition air strike on funeral of Aal al-Rawishan family kills 84 and injures 550 others.

10 October 2016: Taiz, Hadhran, al-Asiqiyah. Suhaib Taufiq Ali Seif is executed by the Houthi-Saleh militia after he refuses to leave his home.

29 October 2016: Taiz, al-Salu district, al-Sharaf village. Coalition air raid on the house of Abdullah al-Shahab results in the death of 11 members of his family: Abdullah al-Shahab (60 years old), his wife Khairiya al-Mansoub (55 years old) and their children Mansour Abdullah al-Shahab (26 years old), Faiza Abdullah al-Shahab (35 years old), Katiba Abdullah al-Shahab (25 years old), Mirvat Abdullah al-Shahab (22 years old), Durriya Abdullah al-Shahab (14 years old), Nasser Abdullah al-Shahab (12 years old), Amro Abdullah al-Shahab (9 years old), Aisha Abdullah al-Shahab (8 years old) and Manar Abdo al-Shahab (8 years old).

4 November 2016: Taiz, Salh district. Deaths of Amani Sadeq al-Awadi (10 years old), Mohammad Shakib Mohammad (9 years old) and Mohammad Hammoud Muqbil (55 years old) in an attack by resistance troops.

14 November 2016: Ibb, Yarim. Coalition air strike on cargo truck kills 12 civilians.

15 November 2016: Sanaa. Walid al-Abi is tortured to death in a Houthi-Saleh militia prison.

16 November 2016: Ibb, Yarim. Coalition air strike on Mahattat al-Qatami neighbourhood kills 25 civilians.

17 November 2016: Taiz, Salh district, Sofitel Market. Six civilians die when a resistance shell hits the market.

23 November 2016: Hajjah, Hayran. Coalition air raid on a truck kills 12 civilians and injures several others.

23 November 2016: Taiz, al-Taiziyya district, al-Thalathin Street. Ahmad Mohammad Said (23 years old) and Ahmad Hassan Abdo (22 years old) are killed by the impact of a Houthi-Saleh militia grenade.

1 December 2016: Ma'rib. Air raid by Coalition kills 7 civilians and injures several others.

1 December 2016: al-Hudaydah, al-Zaidiya district. Sulaiman Yahya Saleh (25 years old), a doctor, dies after being tortured in a Houthi-Saleh militia prison.

7 December 2016: al-Hudaydah, al-Zaidiya district. Mohammad Mohammad Hashibri dies after being tortured in a Houthi-Saleh militia prison.

19 December 2016: Sa'dah, Haidan district. Coalition air raid on a residential building in the Maran area kills 2 women and 5 girls.

19 December 2016: al-Dhalea', Murais district. A Houthi-Saleh militia shell hits the village of al-Ruhba, killing a girl and injuring her mother.

24 December 2016: Ibb, al-Udain, Bab Haiq. Coalition air strike on a home kills 8 civilians, all members of Adnan Ali Masaad's family.

29 December 2016: Taiz, al-Misrakh district, al-Aqrud neighbourhood. Marwan Abdulwahhab (30 years old) is killed by a Houthi-Saleh militia sniper.

30 December 2016: Taiz, Salh district, Sa'ilat al-Qamt neighbourhood. Ibrahim Hammoud (22 years old) and Hussam Hassan Qaed (23 years old) are killed by a Houthi-Saleh militia shell.

9 January 2017: Taiz, Mokha district, Yakhtul. Coalition air raid on ship kills 11 civilians.

10 January 2017: Sanaa, Nihm district, Beni Ma'sar. Coalition air raid on al-Falah School kills 8 students and the principal.

18 January 2017: Taiz, al-Mudhaffar district, Madinat al-Nur neighbourhood. A Houthi-Saleh militia shell explodes, killing 9 civilians: Wahid Mohammad Salam (40 years old), Abdussalam Hassan Abdo al-Salehi (40 years old), Burhan Abdussalam Hassan al-Salehi (21 years old), Salah Abdurrazaq al-Zahri (19 years old), Hissam Adel al-Shumairi (17 years old), Hassan Abdullah al-Rimi (50 years old), Rani Mohammad Mohammad Saleh (20 years old), Hashem Mohammad Mohammad Saleh (27 years old) and Mohammad Hassan Abdullah al-Rimi (15 years old).

19 January 2017: Taiz, al-Mokha district. Coalition air strike on al-Mokha hospital kills 5 civilians.

27 January 2017: Taiz, Bab al-Mandab district, Wahejah. Coalition air strike on Harun Said Mohammad's home kills 4 members of his family.

29 January 2017: al-Bayda', Yakla, al-Gheil village. US-led air strike on al-Dhahab apartment building kills 5 women and 9 children.

11 February 2017: Taiz, al-Mokha district, al-Hali neighbourhood. Coalition air raid on the home of Musa Sultan Abdullah al-Youssefi kills 9 members of his family.

15 February 2017: Sanaa, Arhab district, Shuraa village. Coalition air strike kills 6 of a group of women who had gathered to mourn the dead.

22 February 2017: Taiz, Yakhtul. Coalition air strike on the bridge connecting al-Hudaydah and Taiz kills 7 civilians.

4 March 2017: Taiz, Bab al-Mandab district, Sawabia Island. Coalition air strike on a fishing boat sailing near the island kills 20 fishermen from the al-Khudairi family: Ali Sulaiman Qassem Khudairi, Sulaiman Abdo Murshid Khudairi, Mohammad Abdo Sulaiman Khudairi, Najib Abdo Murshid Khudairi, Hamid Abdo Mohammad Khudairi, Thabet Hassan Mohammad Abdullah Khudairi, Mohammad Ahmad Yahya Salem Khudairi, Abid Sulaiman Qassem Khudairi, Ammar Ahmad Yahya Salem Khudairi, Abdo Sulaiman Qassem Khudairi, Salman Ahmad Hassan Abdo Khudairi, Ahmad Ali Mohammad Said Khudairi, Ali Ahmad Ali Khudairi, Abdo Omar Ali Ahmad Khudairi, Mohammad Salem Ali Khudairi, Anwar Ibrahim Yahya Salem Khudairi, Mohammad Haidar Abid Ahmad Khudairi, Ahmad Hamid Ali Khudairi and Abdullah Muhsen Mohammad Awad Khudairi.

17 March 2017: Ma'rib, Kofel. Twenty-two civilians are killed when a shell fired by Houthi-Saleh militia hits a mosque.

18 March 2017: al-Hudaydah, al-Tair Island. Coalition air strike on a fishing boat kills 9 fishermen: Ali Daoud Ali Battah, Sulaiman Daoud Ali Battah, Said Yahya Marzouq, Hassan Mohammad Ali Mujaji, Abdullah Ali Mahdi, Yahya Mohammad Hammoud Battah, Abid Ibrahim Battah, Mohammad Daoud Ali Battah and Ibrahim Ibrahim al-Sai'iya.

29 March 2017: Taiz, Salh district, al-Askeri neighbourhood. Three children, Anssam Mustafa Mohammad Said (13 years old), Emad Abdulhalim Ahmad (9 years old) and Farah Abdulhalim Ahmad (5 years old) are killed when a Houthi-Saleh militia grenade explodes near them.

4 April 2017: al-Hudaydah, al-Duraihimi. Coalition air raid on coastal strip, kills 4 fishermen.

5 April 2017: al-Jauf, al-Matma district, al-Aula. Coalition air strike on a car driving on highway kills 2 civilians.

5 April 2017: al-Hudaydah, Bajel. Coalition air raid on a straw hut near the salt factory kills 2 civilians.

5 April 2017: Sanaa. The Houthis hold a trial for 36 kidnapped civilians in prison.

8 April 2017: Taiz, al-Mudhaffar district, Wadi al-Salami. A Houthi-Saleh militia shell kills a child and a pregnant woman in the home of Said Mohammad Ghulab.

16 April 2017: Taiz, Mawia Junction. The Houthis execute Omar al-Saidi, an aide in the al-Janad Police Department.

8 May 2017: Taiz, Maqbana district, al-Gheil. Coalition air strike on a car kills 6 civilians.

9 May 2017: Taiz, Maqbana district, al-Barah. Air strike by the Coalition on a house kills all members of the resident family: Bashir Abdullah al-Shumairy, Bashar Abdullah al-Shumairy, Maimuna Abdullah al-Shumairy, Abdullah Bashir Abdullah al-Shumairy and Zawahed Bashir Abdullah al-Shumairy.

13 May 2017: Taiz, Habshi Mountain district, al-Rahba. Three civilians from one family die when a mine laid by Houthi-Saleh militia explodes.

17 May 2017: Aden, Sheikh Othman. Political activist Amjad Abdurrahman Mohammad is murdered by religious extremists.

17 May 2017: Taiz, Muwazzea district, Shaabu exit. Coalition air strike on Mussa Yahya Rajeh's car kills 24 civilians: Mussa Hassan Rajeh, Abdullah Mussa Hassan Rajeh,

Hael Mohammad Hassan Rajeh, Abdulhabib al-Douaihy, Ahmad Abdo Mohammad, Abdulqader Mohammad Said, Mohammad Abdurrahman Haidar, Ibn Hashem Alwan, Ibn Rashed Ali al-Qumairi, Muqbil Salem al-Omairi, Ibrahim Mohammad Salem al-Omairi, Mohammad Hael Hassan Rajeh, Thabet Mohammad Ahmad Qahdan, Saida Mohammad Alwan, Ali Mohammad Hassan, Muqbil Salem Ibrahim, Hashem Alwan al-Rawie, Abdurrahman Haidar, Ahmad Abdo al-Maqhawi, Mukhtar Ali Ghaber and others whose bodies are burned beyond recognition.

19 May 2017: Taiz, al-Mudhaffar district. Safaa Abdulalim, a child, is killed by a Houthi-Saleh militia sniper.

20 May 2017: Taiz, Maqbana district, al-Barah. Coalition air strike on market in al-Barah kills 5 civilians.

20 May 2017: Sanaa, Beit Bus. Coalition air strike on a home kills 2 civilians.

21 May 2017: Taiz, Salh district, al-Humaira. Iman Mohammad al-Sufiani (38 years old) and her son Muhannad Abdullah Abdulhafez (11 years old) are killed after a Houthi-Saleh militia grenade blows up the bus they are on.

21 May 2017: Taiz, Salh district, School of 14 October. Three civilians, Said Ahmad Said (50 years old), Nassar Ammar Ali (13 years old) and Anwar Abdullah Mohammad (38 years old), are killed by a Houthi-Saleh militia shell.

22 May 2017: Taiz, Salh district. A Houthi-Saleh militia shell hits a house occupied by internally displaced persons, killing Abdurrazzaq Ahmad Mulhi (45 years old), father of the resident family, and his wife Sumayya Mahmud Mahdi (35 years old).

22 May 2017: Sanaa Airport. Gunmen belonging to Houthi-Saleh militia open fire on the vehicle of UN envoy Ismail Ould Cheikh.

23 May 2017: Taiz, al-Qahira district. A Houthi-Saleh militia shell kills 5 civilians, including a child: Elias Abdulhakim Qaed (6 years old), Malek Abdurrahman Salem Mohammad (19 years old), Anwar Qaed Hassan Seif (35 years old), Nabil Ali Nasser Mohammad (27 years old) and Salem Mohammad Ali Kaddaf (30 years old).

26 May 2017: Taiz, al-Taiziyya, Mohammad Ali Othman School. Three journalists for the channel al-Ikhbariyya al-Ula: Sa'ad al-Naddari, Taqi Uddin al-Hudhaifi, and cameraman Wael al-Absi are killed by a Houthi-Saleh militia grenade.

29 May 2017: Taiz, al-Mudhaffar district. Fadel Abdussalam Wael (14 years old) is killed by a Houthi-Saleh militia shell.

30 May 2017: Ibb, Hubaish district. Two children are killed by a Houthi sniper.

31 May 2017: Taiz, al-Misrakh, Najd Qusayim. Three civilians, Fares Mohammad Hizaa, Maher Abdulbasset and Bedri Ahmad al-Hajma are killed by a mine laid by Houthi-Saleh militia.

5 June 2017: al-Hudaydah, al-Thawra Hospital. Four kidney patients died from medical supplies shortage as a result of the Coalition-imposed blockade.
6 June 2017: Taiz, al-Qahira district, al-Suwani neighbourhood. Hussein Ali al-Absi and Wael Abdullah Mahiub are killed by the impact of a Houthi-Saleh militia shell.

9 June 2017: Sanaa, al-Khamsin Street. Coalition air strike on Rashad Mohammad al-Mahdi's home kills his wife Daula

Mohammad Hassan al-Dubaili and his children Aliaa Rashad al-Mahdi, Ahmad Rashad al-Mahdi and Jihan Rashad al-Mahdi.

18 June 2017: Sa'dah, border district of Shada. Coalition air strike on Mashnaq market kills 25 civilians and injures several others.

19 June 2017: Taiz. Mohammad Qassem al-Fuhaidi dies after being tortured in a Houthi-Saleh militia prison.

20 June 2017: al-Bayda', al-Zaher district. Two civilians are killed when a Houthi-Saleh militia shell hits the al-Nassefa area.

20 June 2017: al-Hudaydah, al-Thawra Hospital. Two kidney patients die after dialysis centre is unable to continue their treatment as a result of depleted medical supplies.

21 June 2017: Taiz, al-Mudhaffar district, Bir Basha. Two civilians are killed by a Houthi-Saleh militia shell.

24 June 2017: Lahij, al-Qubaita. Ahmad Noaman Ahmad al-Qubbati commits suicide due to the dire economic situation.

25 June 2017: al-Dhalea', Murais district, Ya'is. Two women are killed by a Houthi-Saleh militia shell.

30 June 2017: al-Hudaydah, Haiss Rural Hospital. Two children die of cholera.

30 June 2017: Taiz, Salh district, Kilaba neighbourhood. Ahmad Salah al-Ba'adani (12 years old) is killed by a Houthi-Saleh militia sniper.

1 July 2017: Aden, al-Razi Public Hospital. Manal Said (3 years old) dies of cholera.

3 July 2017: Taiz, al-Mokha district, Yakhtul, Nobat Amer. Coalition air raid on the home of the Halabi family kills 8 family members: Marwan Said Amer (60 years old), Hayat Abdo Ali Ruaidi (40 years old), Saida Abdo Ali Halabi (32 years old), Amani Mohammad Qaed Halabi (12 years old), Soaad Abdo Ali Halabi (11 years old), Ali Abdo Ali Halabi (13 years old), Salem Abdo Ali Halabi (5 years old) and Mariam Abdo Ali Halabi (3 years old).

6 July 2017: Taiz, Maqbana district, al-Barah. Air raid by Coalition kills 8 civilians.

10 July 2017: Taiz, Shar'ab al-Rawna district. The young Saleh Mohammad Ali commits suicide due to the dire economic situation.

17 July 2017: al-Bayda', Radaa. Mukhtar Ali Mohammad al-Ahmadi dies after being tortured in a Houthi-Saleh militia prison.

18 July 2017: Taiz, Muwazzea district, al-Hamili village. Coalition air strike on internally displaced persons kills 20 civilians: Jalila Abd Mohammad al-Bariq, Fathiya Said Ali al-Bariq, Taqwi Said Ali al-Bariq, Sonya Said Ali al-Bariq, Nuria Said Ali al-Bariq, Matera Ali al-Jaum al-Bariq, Faten Muqbil Ali al-Bariq, Marwan Said Ali al-Bariq, Essam Said Ali al-Bariq, Murad Said Ali al-Bariq, Mohammad Said Ali al-Bariq, Ahmad Qaed Jaum al-Bariq, Ali Jaum al-Bariq, Murtada Ali Salem al-Bariq, Jawad Hashem Jaum al-Bariq and 5 others.

21 July 2017: al-Hudaydah, Hanish Island. Coalition shelling of fishing boats kills 8 fishermen: Haitham Yahya Abdurrahman, Qarzua Mohammad Abdullah Fartout,

Omran Said Ali Fartout, Ali Mohammad Dili, Fathi Hassan Asilwa, Hammoud Sulayman Ja'aman, Jawhar Sulayman Ja'aman and Azzeddin Ali Awasi.

22 July 2017: Taiz, Sabr al-Mawadem, al-Shaqab village. Haifa Mohammad Abdulwahhab (5 years old) is killed by a Houthi-Saleh militia grenade.

24 July 2017: Taiz, al-Qahira district, Said riverbed. Recovery of the body of young Mohammad Khalil, who had been murdered then thrown into the riverbed.

26 July 2017: Hajjah, State Political Security prison. Massoud Yahya al-Bukali dies after being kidnapped and tortured in Houthi militia-controlled prison.

29 July 2017: Sanaa. Death of Ahmad, son of political activist Mansur al-Zaila'i, a prisoner in Houthi militia-controlled prison. They didn't allow his father to say goodbye to him.

30 July 2017: Sa'dah, Kattaf district, Jabal al-Central. Coalition air strike on government soldiers kills 14 soldiers.

31 July 2017: al-Hudaydah, al-Thawra Hospital. Death of a sick person in the intensive care unit during a power outage due to lack of fuel resulting from the blockade.

31 July 2017: Taiz, Jabal Habashi, Bilad al-Wafi. Abdo Mohammad al-Wafi dies in al-Khur village at the hands of a Houthi-Saleh militia sniper.

31 July 2017: Taiz, Salh district, al-Thawra Hospital. Mohammad Ali dies while in intensive care during a power outage due to lack of fuel resulting from the blockade.

4 August 2017: Sa'dah, al-Safeiraa district, Mahda. Coalition air strike on a home kills 9 civilians from one family: Huria Abdullah al-Zurafi (50 years old), Sara Ahmad Abdullah al-Zurafi (18 years old), Ummatussalam Ahmad Abdullah al-Zurafi (30 years old), Huria Taha Hussein al-Zurafi (12 years old), Ummaturrazzaq Taha Hussein al-Zurafi (14 years old), Mohammad Taha Hussein al-Zurafi (12 years old), Hassan Taha Hussein al-Zurafi (8 years old), Batul Taha Hussein al-Zurafi (2 years old) and Fatima Taha Hussein al-Zurafi (3 years old).

8 August 2017: Taiz, al-Mudhaffar district, old airport. Death of the pregnant Suad Hassan after Houthi-Saleh militia bombs her home.

8 August 2017: Taiz, al-Qahirah district, Ussaifirah. Hanaa Abdo Abdullah Jasar, a child, dies after being hit by a Houthi-Saleh militia grenade.

27 August 2017: Taiz, al-Mudhaffar district, Nadi al-Saqr. Yasser Abduljalil Mohammad and Assil Nashwan Abduljalil die after being hit by a Houthi-Saleh militia grenade.

28 August 2017: Sanaa. Senior Officer Saleh Mohammad commits suicide due to the dire economic situation.

2 September 2017: Hajjah, Washa district. Coalition air raid on a residential building kills Safia Ahmad al-Maqdi (30 years old), Taqwa Saleh al-Maqdi (40 years old) and Mujrih Walid Hadi al-Maqdi (1 year old).

4 September 2017: Sanaa. Abdullah al-Khumaissi, founder of the Red Crescent in Yemen, dies due to lack of medical supplies in the hospital.

7 September 2017: Ma'rib, al-Rawdah neighbourhood. A woman dies after Houthi-Saleh militia shell a block of flats inhabited by internally displaced persons.

7 September 2017: Sanaa, in front of main entrance of the Political Security Organisation. Ali al-Sudi, father of kidnap victim Mohammad al-Sudi, is killed after a Houthi militia attack.

7 September 2017: Hajjah, Hairan district, al-Sada. Coalition air strike on Hassan al-Hamali's house kills 6 civilians.

8 September 2017: Taiz, al-Waze'iya district, al-Ahiouq. A mine laid by Houthi-Saleh militia blows up and kills 3 civilians: Abdullah al-Haiqi, Hani Salem al-Haiqi and Rida Thabet al-Haiqi.

10 September 2017: Hajjah, Hairan district. Coalition air raid on a weekly market kills 7 civilians.

13 September 2017: Taiz, Sabr al-Mawadem, al-Kassara. Ahmad Mohammad Said dies after Houthi-Saleh militia bomb the al-Nawba village.

14 September 2017: Taiz, al-Salu district, al-Sabhar. A mother and her child die after a mine laid by Houthi-Saleh militia explodes in the Aqaba market.

15 September 2017: Ma'rib, Naqil Shujaa. Coalition air strike on a car kills 12 civilians, including 4 children and 4 women.

15 September 2017: Taiz, Maqbana district, al-Barah. Coalition air strike on a truck in al-Barada area kills 4 civilians: Saleh al-Nahari, Abdullah Ali Sweid, Nabil Mohammad al-Saghir and Ahmad Bujash Aridan.

15 September 2017: Taiz, Salh district, Haud al-Ashraf. Four children die after a Houthi-Saleh militia shell explodes near them: Hammoud Murad al-Salawi (7 years old), Haid Mukhtar Abdulhamid (6 years old), Sarem Samir al-Jabal (9 years old) and Azzam Mohammad Abdullah (11 years old).

18 September 2017: Taiz, Salh district, al-Jahmalia al-Sufla. Four children die in a bombardment by Houthi-Saleh militia: Youssef Khaled Abdulkafi (12 years old), Nasser Mansur Ahmad (14 years old), Rayan Badr Ghaleb (7 years old) and Issa Mohammad al-Humairi (15 years old).

19 September 2017: Hajjah, Hajur. Coalition air raid on a residential building kills Jawhara Ali al-Zira'i and two little girls, Bushra Badr Mohammad al-Zira'i and Amira Mohsen Mohammad al-Zira'i.

27 September 2017: Ibb, Muzaykhira district. Abdo Ahmad Khaled is executed by Houthi-Saleh militia in his own home in front of his family.

28 September 2017: Hajjah, Bakil al-Mir district. Coalition air strike on weekly market; 8 civilians killed or injured.

29 September 2017: Sa'dah, Sahar district. Coalition air strike on a group of workers at a water facility in al-Azqul area kills 8.

29 September 2017: Sa'dah, Razeh. Coalition air raid on two homes kills 1 child and injures several others.

Illustrations

8-9: Nations Online Project (www.nationsonline.org)